# AMERICA
## Militaristic OR Peaceful?

Nate Reztirob

# AMERICA
## Militaristic OR Peaceful?

**Nate Reztirob**

America: Militaristic or Peaceful?
by Nate Reztirob

First edition 2023



ISBN 978-09910083-6-0

*Veronica Lane Books*
www.veronicalanebooks.com
*Books That Make a Difference*

11420 US-1, Suite 124, N. Palm Beach, FL 33408 USA
Tel: +1(833) VLBOOKS (+1 833-852-6657)

# Table of Contents


Chapter 1 What is Peace?....................................................2

Chapter 2 Love, Friendship, and Peace.............................32

Chapter 3 Pax Americana....................................................57

Chapter 4 The Costs of American Militarism vs. Peace: Constructive Solutions.........................................149

Chapter 5 Is America Corrupt?..........................................193

About the Author................................................................255

# Chapter 1

# What is Peace?

What is Peace? Is peace something outside of us, or is peace something inside us? Is peace something you can learn, or is peace something we are born with? Is peace something we can do, or is peace just a feeling? Or, is peace both a feeling and something we can do? Maybe peace is a real nice awake kind of feeling, not like being excited and playing, but not like being sleepy either. Maybe peace is a nice kind of feeling, like just lying on your back and watching the clouds go by. – Children's Book

## Etymology[1]

The term 'peace'[2] originates most recently from the Anglo-French *pes,* and the Old French *pais*, meaning "peace, reconciliation, silence, agreement" (11th century). The Anglo-French term *pes* itself comes from the Latin *pax*, meaning "peace, compact, agreement, treaty of peace, tranquility, absence of hostility, harmony." The English word came into use in various personal

---

[1] "Spiritual Life Coaching: Najaam Lee's Healng Tempal," NAJAAM LEE'S HEALNG, https://www.najaamlee.com/.

[2] "The Spiritual Life Windows to Spirituality," The Spiritual Life, https://slife.org/.

greetings from c.1300 as a translation of the Hebrew word *shalom*, which, according to Jewish theology, comes from a Hebrew verb meaning 'to be complete, whole'.

Although 'peace' is the usual translation, however, it is an incomplete one, because '*shalom*,' which is also cognate with the Arabic *salaam*, has multiple other meanings in addition to peace, including justice, good health, safety, well-being, prosperity, equity, security, good fortune, and friendliness, as well as simply the greetings, "hello" and "goodbye." On a personal level, peaceful behaviors are kind, considerate, respectful, just, and tolerant of others' beliefs and behaviors – tending to manifest goodwill.

This latter understanding of peace can also pertain to an individual's introspective sense or concept of her/himself, as in being "at peace" in one's own mind, as found in European references from c.1200. The early English term is also used in the sense of "quiet," reflecting calm, serene, and meditative approaches to family or group relationships that avoid quarreling and seek tranquility — an absence of disturbance or agitation.

In many languages, the word for peace is also used as a greeting or a farewell, for example, the Hawaiian word *aloha*, In English, peace is occasionally used as a farewell, especially for the dead, as in the phrase *rest in peace*.

## Ideological Beliefs of Peace

# Pacifism[3]

Pacifism is the categorical opposition to the behaviors of war or violence as a means of settling disputes or of gaining advantage. Pacifism covers a spectrum of views ranging from the belief that international disputes can and should all be resolved via peaceful behaviors; to calls for the abolition of various organizations which tend to institutionalize aggressive behaviors, such as the military, or arms manufacturers; to opposition to any organization of society that might rely in any way upon governmental force. Such groups which sometimes oppose the governmental use of force include anarchists and libertarians. Absolute pacifism opposes violent behavior under all circumstances, including the defense of self and others.

Pacifism may be based on moral principles (a deontological view) or pragmatism (a consequentialist view). Principled pacifism holds that all forms of violent behavior are inappropriate responses to conflict and are morally wrong. Pragmatic pacifism holds that the costs of war and interpersonal violence are so substantial that better ways of resolving disputes must be found.

---

3 "Peace," Wikiwand, https://www.wikiwand.com/en/Peace.

## Inner Peace, Meditation and Prayerfulness

Psychological or inner peace (i.e. peace of mind) refers to a state of being internally or spiritually at peace, with sufficient knowledge and understanding to keep oneself calm in the face of apparent discord or stress. Being internally "at peace"[4] is considered by many to be a healthy mental state, or homeostasis and to be the opposite of feeling stressful, mentally anxious, or emotionally unstable. Within the meditative traditions, the psychological or inward achievement of "peace of mind" is often associated with bliss and happiness.

Peace of mind, serenity, and calmness are descriptions of a disposition free from the effects of stress. In some meditative traditions[5], inner peace is believed to be a state of consciousness or enlightenment that may be cultivated by various types of meditation, prayer, ***t'ai chi ch'uan*** (**太极拳**, ***tàijíquán***), yoga, or other various types of mental or physical disciplines. Many such practices refer to this peace as an experience of knowing oneself. An emphasis on finding one's inner peace is often associated with traditions such as Buddhism, Hinduism, and some traditional Christian contemplative practices such as monasticism, as well as with the New Age movement.

---

[4] "Peace: Natural Bach Flower Remedies: Order Now," Natural Bach Flower Remedies, February 13, 2019, https://www.drbfr.com/peace/.

[5] Andrew Marshall, "What Is Peace?," Boot Camp & Military Fitness Institute, https://bootcampmilitaryfitnessinstitute.com/2022/09/09/what-is-peace-2/.

## Non-Aggression Principle

The Non-Aggression Principle (NAP)[6] asserts that aggression against an individual or an individual's property is always an immoral violation of one's life, liberty, and property rights. Utilizing deceit instead of consent to achieve ends is also a violation of the Non-Aggression principle. Therefore, under the framework of the Non-Aggression principle, rape, murder, deception, involuntary taxation, government regulation, and other behaviors that initiate aggression against otherwise peaceful individuals are considered violations of this principle. This principle is most commonly adhered to by libertarians. A common elevator pitch for this principle is, "Good ideas don't require force."

## Satyagraha

Satyagraha is a philosophy and practice of nonviolent resistance developed by Mohandas Gandhi. He deployed *satyagraha*[7] techniques in campaigns for Indian independence and also during his earlier struggles in South Africa.

The word *satyagraha* itself was coined through a public contest that Gandhi sponsored through the newspaper he published in South Africa, *Indian Opinion*, when he realized that neither the common,

---

[6] Andrew Marshall, "What Is Peace?," Boot Camp & Military Fitness Institute, https://bootcampmilitaryfitnessinstitute.com/2022/09/09/what-is-peace-2/.

[7] "What Is Satyagraha?" Gandhi Development Trust, November 9, 2017, https://www.gdt.org.za/gdt/what-is-satyagraha/.

contemporary Hindu language nor the English language contained a word which fully expressed his own meanings and intentions when he talked about his nonviolent approaches to conflict. According to a 'truth-firmness', and is commonly translated as 'steadfastness in the truth' or 'truth-force'.

Satyagraha theory also influenced Martin Luther King Jr., James Bevel, and others during the campaigns they led during the civil rights movement in the United States. The theory of *satyagraha* sees means and ends to peace as inseparable. Therefore, it is contradictory to try to use violence to obtain peace. As Gandhi wrote: “I would say, 'means are everything'. As the expression goes: “The means to the end..." Gandhi sums it up: "There is no way to peace; peace is the way.”

## History of Peace

Throughout history, victors have sometimes used ruthless measures to impose peace upon the vanquished. In his book *Agricola,* the Roman historian Tacitus includes eloquent and vicious polemics against the rapacity and greed of Rome[8]. One, that Tacitus says is by the Caledonian chieftain Calgacus, ends with: *Auferre trucidare rapere falsis nominibus imperium, atque ubi solitudinem faciunt, pacem appellant.* (To ravage, to slaughter, to usurp under false titles, they call empire; and where they make a desert, they call it peace. — Oxford Revised Translation).

---

[8] “Greed in a Simple Plan by Alfred A. Knopf,” Bartleby, https://www.bartleby.com/essay/Greed-in-a-Simple-Plan-by-Alfred-PKVCA44CDB6A.

Discussion of peace is therefore at the same time a discussion on its form. Is it simply the absence of mass organized killing (war), or does peace require a particular morality and justice? (*just peace*). A peace must be seen at least in two forms:

- A simple silence of arms, absence of war.
- Absence of is war accompanied by particular requirements for the mutual settlement of relations, which are characterized by terms such as justice, mutual respect, and respect for law and goodwill.[9]

More recently, advocates for radical reform in justice systems have called for a public policy adoption of non-punitive, non-violent Restorative Justice methods. Many of those studying the success of these methods, including a United Nations working group on Restorative Justice Archived 26 July 2011 at the Wayback Machine, have attempted to re-define justice in terms related to peace. From the late 2000s on, a Theory of Active Peace has been proposed that conceptually integrates justice into a larger peace theory.

Another internationally important approach to peace is the international, national and local protection of cultural assets in the event of conflicts. United Nations, UNESCO, and Blue Shield International deal with the protection of cultural heritage. This also applies to the integration of United Nations peacekeeping. UNESCO Director-General Irina Bokova stated: "The protection of culture and heritage is a humanitarian and security policy imperative

---

[9] Andrew Marshall, "What Is Peace?" Boot Camp & Military Fitness Institute https://bootcampmilitaryfitnessinstitute.com/2022/09/09/what-is-peace-2/.

that also paves the way for resilience, reconciliation, and peace." The protection of the cultural heritage should preserve the particularly sensitive cultural memory, the growing cultural diversity, and the economic basis of a state, a municipality, or a region. In many conflicts, there is a deliberate attempt to destroy the opponent's cultural heritage. Whereby there is also a connection between cultural user disruption or cultural heritage and the cause of flight. However, protection can only be implemented in a sustainable manner through the fundamental cooperation and training of military units and civilian personnel, together with the locals. The president of Blue Shield International Karl von Habsburg summed it up with the words: “Without the local community and without the local participants, that would be completely impossible.”

## Peace Theories[10]

Many different theories of "peace" exist in the world of peace studies, which involves the study of de-escalation, conflict transformation, disarmament, and cessation of violence. The definition of "peace" can vary with religion, culture, or subject of study.

### Socialism and Managed Capitalism

Socialist, communist, and left-wing liberal writers of the 19th and 20th

---

[10] “Peace Facts for Kids,” Peace Facts for Kids, https://kids.kiddle.co/Peace.

centuries (e.g., Lenin, J.A. Hobson, John Strachey)[11] argued that capitalism caused war (e.g. through promoting imperial or other economic rivalries that lead to international conflict). This led some to argue that international socialism was the key to peace.

## Free trade and Interdependence

It was a central tenet of classical liberalism, for example among English liberal thinkers of the late 19th and early 20th century, that free trade promoted peace. For example, the Cambridge economist John Maynard Keynes (1883–1946) said that he was "brought up" on this idea and held it unquestioned until at least the 1920s. During the economic globalization in the decades leading up to World War I, writers such as Norman Angell argued that the growth of economic interdependence between the great powers made war between them futile and therefore unlikely. He made this argument in 1913. A year later Europe's economically interconnected states were embroiled in what would later become known as the First World War.

## Balance of Power

The classical "realist" position is that the key to promoting order between states, and so of increasing the chances of peace, is the maintenance of a balance of power between states – a situation where no state is so dominant that it can "lay down the law to the rest". Exponents of this view have included Metternich, Bismarck,

---

[11] Upender Singh, *Battalion Command: Dare to Lead* (New Delhi: Neha Publishers & Distributors, 2022), 206.

Hans Morgenthau, and Henry Kissinger. A related approach – more in the tradition of Hugo Grotius than Thomas Hobbes – was articulated by the so-called "English school of international relations theory"[12] such as Martin Wight in his book *Power Politics* (1946, 1978) and Hedley Bull in *The Anarchical Society* (1977).

However, in response to such writers in the 1930s who argued that capitalism caused war, the economist John Maynard Keynes (1883–1946) argued that managed capitalism could promote peace. This involved international coordination of fiscal/monetary policies, an international monetary system that did not pit the interests of countries against each other, and a high degree of freedom of trade. These ideas underlay Keynes's work during World War II that led to the creation of the International Monetary Fund and the World Bank at Bretton Woods in 1944, and later of the General Agreement on Tariffs and Trade (subsequently the World Trade Organization).

In the second half of the 20th century, and especially during the cold war, a particular form of balance of power – mutual nuclear deterrence – emerged as a widely held doctrine on the key to peace between the great powers. Critics argued that the development of nuclear stockpiles increased the chances of war rather than peace, and that the "nuclear umbrella" made it "safe" for smaller wars (e.g. the Vietnam war and the Soviet invasion of Czechoslovakia to end the Prague Spring), so making such wars more likely.

---

[12] Upender Singh, *Battalion Command: Dare to Lead* (New Delhi: Neha Publishers & Distributors, 2022), 205.

## Territorial Peace Theory

The territorial peace theory posits that peace causes democracy because territorial wars between neighbor countries lead to authoritarian attitudes and disregard for democratic values. This theory is supported by historical studies showing that countries rarely become democratic until after their borders have been settled by territorial peace with neighbor countries.

## The Peace and War Game

The *Peace and War Game*[13] is an approach in game theory to understand the relationship between peace and conflicts.

The iterated game hypotheses were originally used by academic groups and computer simulations to study possible strategies of cooperation and peacemakers became richer over time, it became clear that making war had greater costs than initially anticipated. One of the well-studied strategies that acquired wealth more rapidly was based on Genghis Khan, i.e. a constant aggressor making war continually to gain resources. This led, in contrast, to the development of what's known as the "provokable nice guy strategy", a peace-maker until attacked, improved upon merely to win by occasional forgiveness even when attacked. By adding the results of all pairwise games for each player, one sees that multiple players gain wealth cooperating with each other while bleeding a constantly

[13] "Peace War Game," Wikipedia (Wikimedia Foundation, October 31, 2021), https://en.wikipedia.org/wiki/Peace_war_game.

aggressive player.

## International Organization and Law

One of the most influential theories of peace, especially since Woodrow Wilson led the creation of the League of Nations at the Paris Peace Conference of 1919[14], is that peace will be advanced if the intentional anarchy of states is replaced through the growth of international law promoted and enforced through international organizations such as the League of Nations, the United Nations, and other functional international organizations. One of the most important early exponents of this view was Alfred Eckhart Zimmern, for example in his 1936 book *The League of Nations and the Rule of Law.*

## Trans-National Solidarity

Many "idealist" thinkers about international relations – e.g. in the traditions of Kant and Karl Marx – have argued that the key to peace is the growth of some form of solidarity between peoples (or classes of people) spanning the lines of cleavage between nations or states that lead to war.

One version of this is the idea of promoting international understanding between nations through the international mobility of students – an idea most powerfully advanced by Cecil Rhodes in the creation of the Rhodes Scholarships, and his successors such as J.

---

[14] Upender Singh, *Battalion Command: Dare to Lead* (New Delhi: Neha Publishers & Distributors, 2022), 207

William Fulbright.[15]

Another theory is that peace can be developed among countries on the basis of active management of water resources.

## Peace Day

Peace day was founded as a day to recognize, honor and promote peace. It is commemorated each year on September 21st by United Nations members. The United Nations established International Peace Day in 1981 with the first observance held on September 21, 1982. Each year, the UN emphasizes a different theme. Some of the past themes have included: Climate Action for Peace (2019)

## Peace Organizations and Prizes

### United Nations

The United Nations (UN) is an international organization whose stated aims are to facilitate cooperation in international law, international security, economic development, social progress, human rights, and achieving world peace[16]. The UN was founded in 1945 after World War II to replace the League of Nations, to stop wars between countries, and to provide a platform for dialogue.

After authorization by the Security Council, the UN sends

---

[15] Andrew Marshall, "What Is Peace?" Boot Camp & Military Fitness Institute, September 9, 2022, https://bootcampmilitaryfitnessinstitute.com/2022/09/09/what-is-peace-2/.

[16] "United Nations," Left Behind Wiki, https://leftbehind.fandom.com/wiki/United_Nations.

peacekeepers to regions where armed conflict has recently ceased or paused to enforce the terms of peace agreements and to discourage combatants from resuming hostilities. Since the UN does not maintain its own military, peacekeeping forces are voluntarily provided by member states of the UN. The forces, also called the "Blue Helmets," who enforce UN accords are awarded United Nations Medals, which are considered international decorations instead of military decorations. The peacekeeping force as a whole received the Nobel Peace Prize in 1988.

## Police

The obligation of the state to provide for domestic peace within its borders in usually charged to the police and other general domestic policing activities.[17] The police are a constituted body of persons empowered by a state to enforce the law, to protect the lives, liberty and possessions of citizens, and to prevent crime and civil disorder. Their powers include the power of arrest and the legitimized use of force. The term is most commonly associated with the police forces of a sovereign state that are authorized to exercise the police power of that state within a defined legal or territorial area of responsibility. Police forces are often defined as being separate from the military and other organizations involved in the defense of the state against foreign aggressors; however, gendarmerie are military units charged with civil policing. Police forces are usually public sector services,

---

[17] "United Nations Peacekeeping," United Nations (United Nations), https://peacekeeping.un.org/en.

funded through taxes.

## National Security

It is the obligation of national security to provide for peace and security in a nation against foreign threats and foreign aggression. Potential causes of national insecurity include actions by other states (e.g. military or cyberattack), violent non-state actors (e.g. terrorist attack), organized criminal groups such as narcotic cartels, and also the effects of natural disasters (e.g. flooding, earthquakes). Systemic drivers of insecurity, which may be transnational, include climate change, economic inequality and marginalization, political exclusion, and militarization. In view of the wide range of risks, the preservation of peace and the security of a nation state have several dimensions, including economic security, energy security, physical security, environmental security, food security, border security, and cyber security. These dimensions correlate closely with elements of national power.

## League of Nations

The principal forerunner of the United Nations was the League of Nations. It was created at the Paris Peace Conference of 1919, and emerged from the advocacy of Woodrow Wilson and other idealists during World War I. The Covenant of the League of Nations was included in the Treaty of Versailles in 1919, and the League was based in Geneva until its dissolution as a result of World War II and replacement by the United Nations. The high hopes widely held for the League in the 1920s, for example amongst members of the

League of Nations Union, gave way to widespread disillusion in the 1930s as the League struggled to respond to challenges from Nazi Germany, Fascist Italy, and Japan.

One of the most important scholars of the League of Nations was Sir Alfred Eckhard Zimmern. Like many of the other British enthusiasts for the League, such as Gilbert Murray and Florence Stawell – known as the "Greece and peace" set – he came to this from the study of the classics[18].

The creation of the League of Nations[19], and the hope for informed public opinion on international issues (expressed for example by the Union for Democratic Control during World War I), also saw the creation after World War I of bodies dedicated to understanding international affairs, such as the Council on Foreign Relations in New York and the Royal Institute of International Affairs at Chatham House in London. At the same time, the academic study of international relations started to professionalize, with the creation of the first professorship of international politics, named for Woodrow Wilson, at Aberystwyth, Wales, in 1919.

## Nobel Peace Prize

The highest honor awarded to peacemakers is the Nobel Prize in Peace, awarded since 1901 by the Norwegian Nobel Committee. It is awarded annually to internationally notable persons following the

---

[18] "Peace," Wikipedia (Wikimedia Foundation, October 19, 2022), https://en.wikipedia.org/wiki/Peace.

[19] Upender Singh, *Battalion Command: Dare to Lead* (New Delhi: Neha Publishers & Distributors, 2022),199.

prize's creation in the will of Alfred Nobel[20]. According to Nobel's will, the Peace Prize shall be awarded to the person who "...shall have done the most or the best work for fraternity between nations, for the abolition or reduction of standing armies, and for the holding and promotion of peace congresses."[21]

## Olympic Games

The late 19th-century idealist advocacy of peace which led to the creation of the Nobel Peace Prize, the Rhodes Scholarships, the Carnegie Endowment for International Peace, and ultimately the League of Nations, also saw the re-emergence of the ancient Olympic ideal. Led by Pierre de Coubertin, this culminated in the holding in 1896 of the first of the modern Olympic Games.

## Rhodes, Fulbright and Schwarzman Scholarships

In creating the Rhodes Scholarships for outstanding students from the United States, Germany and much of the British Empire, Cecil Rhodes wrote in 1901 that 'the object is that an understanding between the three great powers will render war impossible and educational relations make the strongest tie.' This peace purpose of the Rhodes Scholarships was very prominent in the first half of the 20th century, and became prominent again in recent years under

---

[20] "Alfred Nobel's Will," NobelPrize.org, May 24, 2021, https://www.nobelprize.org/alfred-nobel/alfred-nobels-will/.

[21] "POLSC101: Introduction to Political Science," Saylor Academy, https://learn.saylor.org/course/POLSC101.

Warden of the Rhodes House Donald Markwell, a historian of thought about the causes of war and peace. This vision greatly influenced Senator J. William Fulbright in the goal of the Fulbright fellowships to promote international understanding and peace, and has guided many other international fellowship programs, including the Schwarzman Scholars to China created by Stephen A. Schwarzman in 2013.

## Gandhi Peace Prize[22]

The International Gandhi Peace Prize, named after Mahatma Gandhi, is awarded annually by the Government of India. It was launched as a tribute to the ideals espoused by Gandhi in 1995 on the occasion of the 125th anniversary of his birth. This is an annual award given to individuals and institutions for their contributions toward social, economic and, political transformation through non-violence and other Gandhian methods. The award carries Rs. 10 million in cash, convertible in any currency in the world, a plaque, and a citation. It is open to all persons regardless of nationality, race, creed, or sex.

## Student Peace Prize

The Student Peace Prize is a UN awarded biennially to a student or a student organization that has made a significant contribution to

---

[22] "Gandhi Peace Prize," Wikipedia (Wikimedia Foundation, May 26, 2022), https://en.wikipedia.org/wiki/Gandhi_Peace_Prize.

promoting peace and human rights.

## Culture of Peace News Network

The Culture of Peace News Network, otherwise known simply as CPNN, is a UN-authorized interactive online news network, committed to supporting the global movement for a culture of peace.

## Sydney Peace Prize

Every year in the first week of November, the Sydney Peace Foundation presents the Sydney Peace Prize.[23] The Sydney Peace Prize is awarded to an organization or an individual whose life and work has demonstrated significant contributions to:

The achievement of peace with justice locally, nationally or internationally
The promotion and attainment of human rights
The philosophy, language and practice of non-violence

## Peace Museums

A peace museum is a museum that documents historical peace initiatives. Many provide advocacy programs for nonviolent conflict resolution. This may include conflicts at the personal, regional or

---

[23] "Sydney Peace Prize," Sydney Peace Foundation, February 20, 2022, https://sydneypeacefoundation.org.au/sydney-peace-prize/.

international level.

Smaller institutions include the Randolph Bourne Institute, the McGill Middle East Program of Civil Society and Peace Building and the International Festival of Peace Poetry.

## Religious Beliefs Regarding Peace

People often seek to identify and address the basic problems of human life, including conflicts between, among, and within persons and societies. In ancient Greek-speaking areas, the virtue of peace was personified as the goddess Eirene, and in Latin-speaking areas as the goddess *Pax*. Her image was typically represented by ancient sculptors as a full-grown woman, usually with a horn of plenty and scepter and sometimes with a torch or olive leaves.

### Christianity

Christians, who believe Jesus of Nazareth to be the Jewish Messiah called Christ (meaning Anointed One), interpret Isaiah 9:6 as a messianic prophecy of Jesus in which he is called the "Prince of Peace." In the Gospel of Luke, Zechariah celebrates his son John: And you, child, will be called prophet of the Most High, for you will go before the Lord to prepare his ways, to give his people knowledge of salvation through the forgiveness of their sins, because of the tender mercy of our God by which the daybreak from on high will visit us to shine on those who sit in darkness and death's shadow, to guide our feet into the path of peace[24].

As a testimony of peace, Churches of the Anabaptist Christian tradition (such as the Mennonites), as well Holiness Methodist Pacifists (such as the Immanuel Missionary Church) and Quakers (such as the Conservative Friends), practice nonresistance and do not participate in warfare.

In the Catholic Church, numerous pontifical documents on the Holy Rosary document a continuity of views of the Popes to have confidence in the Holy Rosary as a means to foster peace. Subsequently, to the Encyclical Mense1965, in which he urged the practice of the Holy Rosary, "the prayer so dear to the Virgin and so much recommended by the Supreme Pontiffs," and as reaffirmed in the encyclical Christi Matri, 1966, to implore peace, Pope Paul VI stated in the apostolic *Recurrens mensis*, October 1969, that the Rosary is a prayer that favors the great gift of peace.

## Hinduism

Hindu texts contain the following passages related to peace:

> May there be peace in the heavens, peace in the atmosphere, peace on the earth. Let there be coolness in the water, healing in the herbs and peace radiating from the trees. Let there be harmony in the planets and in the stars, and perfection in eternal knowledge. May everything in the universe be at peace. Let peace pervade

---

24 "Our Patron - Our Mission," CatholicTherapists.com, https://www.catholictherapists.com/our-patron-our-mission.

everywhere, at all times. May I experience that peace within my own heart.

*— Yajur Veda 36.17*

Let us have concord with our own people, and concord with people who are strangers to us. Ashwins (Celestial Twins,)[25] create between us and the strangers a unity of hearts. May we unite in our minds, unite in our purposes, and not fight against the heavenly spirit within us. Let not the battle-cry rise amidst many slain, nor the arrows of the war-god fall with the break of day.

*— Yajur Veda 7.52*

A superior being does not render evil for evil. This is a maxim one should observe... One should never harm the wicked or the good or even animals meriting death. A noble soul will exercise compassion even towards those who enjoy injuring others or cruel deeds... Who is without fault?

*— Valmiki, Ramayana*

The chariot that leads to victory is of another kind. Valor and fortitude are its wheels;Truthfulness and virtuous conduct are its banner; Strength, discretion, self-restraint and benevolence are its four horses, Harnessed with the

---

[25] "Hindu, Hinduism and Hindustan: Part LXXIII by Jaipal Singh," Boloji.com, https://www.boloji.com/articles/53396/hindu-hinduism-and-hindustan-part-lxxiii.

cords of forgiveness, compassion and equanimity... Whoever has this righteous chariot, has no enemy to conquer anywhere.

— *Valmiki, Ramayana*

## Buddhism

Buddhists believe that peace can be attained once all suffering ends. They regard all suffering as stemming from cravings (in the extreme, greed), aversions (fears), or delusions[26]. To eliminate such suffering and achieve personal peace, followers in the path of the Buddha adhere to a set of teachings called the Four Noble Truths — a central tenet in Buddhist philosophy.

## Islam

Islam derived from the root word *salam* which literally means peace. Muslims are called followers of Islam. Quran clearly stated "Those who have believed and whose hearts are assured by the remembrance of Allah. Unquestionably, by the remembrance of Allah, hearts are assured" and stated "O you who have believed, when you are told, "Space yourselves" in assemblies, then make space; Allah will make space for you. And when you are told, "Arise," then arise; Allah will raise those who have believed among you and

---

[26] Ven Dr Sumedh Thero, *Meditation for World Peace* (Scholars' Press, 2018).

those who were given knowledge, by degrees[27]. And Allah is acquainted with what you do."

## Judaism

The Judaic tradition directly associates God with peace, as evidenced by various principles and laws in Judaism. *Shalom*, the biblical and modern Hebrew word for peace, is one of the names for God according to the Judaic law and tradition. For instance, in traditional Jewish law, individuals are prohibited from saying "Shalom" when they are in the bathroom as there is a prohibition on uttering any of God's names in the bathroom, out of respect for the divine name. Jewish liturgy and prayer is replete with prayers asking God to establish peace in the world. The *Shmoneh Esreh*, a key prayer in Judaism that is recited three times each day, concludes with a blessing for peace. The last blessing of the *Shmoneh Esreh*, also known as the *Amida* ("standing" as the prayer is said while standing), is focused on peace, beginning and ending with supplications for peace and blessings. Peace is central to Judaism's core principle of *Moshiach* ("messiah") which connotes a time of universal peace and abundance, a time where weapons will be turned into plowshares and lions will sleep with lambs. As it is written in the Book of Isaiah 2:4 and 11:6-9:

> They shall beat their swords into plowshares and their spears into pruning hooks; nation will not lift sword against

---

[27] Sahih International et al., "Surah Mujadila Ayat 11 (58:11 Quran) with Tafsir," My Islam, https://myislam.org/surah-mujadila/ayat-11/.

nation and they will no longer study warfare.

The wolf will live with the lamb, the leopard will lie down with the goat, the calf and the lion and the yearling together; and a little child will lead them. The cow will feed with the bear, their young will lie down together, and the lion will eat straw like the ox[28]. The infant will play near the hole of the cobra, and the young child put his hand into the viper's nest. They will neither harm nor destroy on all my holy mountain, for the earth will be full of the knowledge of the Lord as the waters cover the sea.

This last metaphor from *Tanakh* (Hebrew bible) symbolizes the peace that a longed for messianic age will be characterized by, a peace where natural enemies, the strong and the weak, predator and prey, will live in harmony.

Jews pray for the messianic age of peace every day in the *Shmoneh Esreh* in addition to faith in the coming of the messianic age constituting one of the thirteen core principles of faith in Judaism, according to Maimonides.

Studies, Rankings, and Periods

## Peace and Conflict Studies

*Peace and conflict studies* is an academic field which identifies and analyses violent and nonviolent behaviors, as well as the structural

[28] Isaiah 11:7 the cow will graze with the bear, their young will lie down together, and the lion will eat straw like the ox., https://biblehub.com/isaiah/11-7.htm.

mechanisms attending violent and non-violent social conflicts. This is to better understand the processes leading to a more desirable human condition. One variation, *Peace studies* (*irenology*), is an interdisciplinary effort aiming at the prevention, de-escalation, and solution of conflicts. This contrasts with war studies (*polemology*), directed at the efficient attainment of victory in conflicts. Disciplines involved may include political science, geography, economics, psychology, sociology, international relations, history, anthropology, religious studies, and gender studies, as well as a variety of other disciplines.

## Measurement and Ranking of Peace

Although peace is widely perceived as something intangible, various organizations have been making efforts to quantify and measure it. The Global Peace Index produced by the Institute for Economics and Peace is a known effort to evaluate peacefulness in countries based on 23 indicators of the absence of violence and absence of the fear of violence.

The last edition of the Index ranks 163 countries on their internal and external levels of peace. According to the 2017 Global Peace Index, Iceland is the most peaceful country in the world while Syria is the least peaceful one. Fragile States Index (formerly known as the Failed States Index) created by the Fund for Peace focuses on risk for instability or violence in 178 nations. This index measures how fragile a state is by 12 indicators and sub-indicators that evaluate aspects of politics, social economy, and military facets in countries. The 2015 Failed State Index reports that the most fragile nation is

South Sudan, and the least fragile one is Finland. University of Maryland publishes the Peace and Conflict Instability Ledger in order to measure peace. It grades 163 countries with 5 indicators and pays the most attention to the risk of political instability or armed conflict over a three-year period. The most recent ledger shows that the most peaceful country is Slovenia; on the contrary Afghanistan is the most conflicted nation. Besides indicated above reports from the Institute for Economics and Peace, Fund for Peace, and the University of Maryland, other organizations including George Mason University release indexes that rank countries in terms of peacefulness.

## Longest Periods of Peace

The longest continuing period of peace and neutrality among currently existing states is observed in Sweden since 1814, and in Switzerland, which has had an official policy of neutrality since 1815. This was made possible partly by the periods of relative peace in Europe and the world known as Pax Britannica (1815–1914), Pax Europaea/Pax Americana (since 1950s), and Pax Atomica (also since the 1950s).

What is Peace? Did you ever go someplace real quiet like a deep green forest, or a hot dry desert, or up on a really high mountain? If you ever go to one of those places and you stop talking and playing around, if you can stand or sit really still, just for a few minutes, maybe you can *feel* peace there. But do you have to go to a quiet place, far from the city with all the cars and people and noise and crazy stuff going on, to feel peace? Maybe we are born with peace already deep inside us, and maybe we can feel the peace that is already deep inside us—anywhere!

## Bibliography

"Alfred Nobel's Will." NobelPrize.org, May 24, 2021. https://www.nobelprize.org/alfred-nobel/alfred-nobels-will/.

"Gandhi Peace Prize." Wikipedia. Wikimedia Foundation, May 26, 2022. https://en.wikipedia.org/wiki/Gandhi_Peace_Prize.

"Greed in a Simple Plan by Alfred A. Knopf." Bartleby. https://www.bartleby.com/essay/Greed-in-a-Simple-Plan-by-Alfred-PKVCA44CDB6A.

"Hindu, Hinduism and Hindustan: Part LXXIII by Jaipal Singh." Boloji.com. https://www.boloji.com/articles/53396/hindu-hinduism-and-hindustan-part-lxxiii.

International, Sahih, Yusuf Ali, Abul Ala Maududi, Muhsin Khan, Pickthall, Dr. Ghali, and Abdel Haleem. "Surah Mujadila Ayat 11 (58:11 Quran) with Tafsir." My Islam. https://myislam.org/surah-mujadila/ayat-11/.

Isaiah 11:7 the cow will graze with the bear, their young will lie down together, and the lion will eat straw like the ox. Accessed October 25, 2022. https://biblehub.com/isaiah/11-7.htm.

Marshall, Andrew. "What Is Peace?" Boot Camp & Military Fitness Institute, September 9, 2022. https://bootcampmilitaryfitnessinstitute.com/2022/09/09/what-is-peace-2/.

"Our Patron - Our Mission." CatholicTherapists.com. https://www.catholictherapists.com/our-patron-our-mission.

"Peace Facts for Kids." Peace Facts for Kids. https://kids.kiddle.co/Peace.

"Peace: Natural Bach Flower Remedies: Order Now." Natural Bach Flower Remedies, February 13, 2019. https://www.drbfr.com/peace/.

"Peace." Wikipedia. Wikimedia Foundation, October 19, 2022. https://en.wikipedia.org/wiki/Peace.

"Peace." Wikiwand. https://www.wikiwand.com/en/Peace.

"Peace War Game." Wikipedia. Wikimedia Foundation, October 31, 2021. https://en.wikipedia.org/wiki/Peace_war_game.

"POLSC101: Introduction to Political Science." Saylor Academy. https://learn.saylor.org/course/POLSC101.

Singh, Upender. *Battalion Command: Dare to Lead.* New Delhi: Neha Publishers & Distributors, 2020.

"Spiritual Life Coaching: Najaam Lee's Healng Tempal." NAJAAM LEE'S HEALNG. https://www.najaamlee.com/.

"Sydney Peace Prize." Sydney Peace Foundation, February 20, 2022. https://sydneypeacefoundation.org.au/sydney-peace-prize/.

"The Spiritual Life Windows to Spirituality." The Spiritual Life. 2022. https://slife.org/.

Thero, Ven Dr Sumedh. *Meditation for World Peace*. Scholars' Press, 2018.

"United Nations." Left Behind Wiki. Accessed October 25, 2022. https://leftbehind.fandom.com/wiki/United_Nations.

"United Nations Peacekeeping." United Nations. United Nations. https://peacekeeping.un.org/en.

"What Is Satyagraha?" Gandhi Development Trust, November 9, 2017. . https://www.gdt.org.za/gdt/what-is-satyagraha/.

# Chapter 2

# Love, Friendship, and Respect

Peace is comprised of many different elements. Let's take up three of the most important aspects that help people to live peaceful lives personally and in society: Love, Friendship, and Respect. One must strive to understand these principal qualities and then make every attempt to practice these merits in their daily life.

## Love

> Love is the biggest inside feeling that anyone can ever have! All the different inside feelings we have are like the different colors inside a rainbow- Feeling sad is like a blue color. Feeling happy is like a yellow color. Feeling angry is like a red color. But Love is our *biggest* inside feeling! All the different inside feelings we have are held together by Love just like a rainbow holds together all the different colors inside of it.
>
> \- Children's Story

We can begin to define Love as the ancient Greeks did, using several different words for love, enabling them to distinguish more clearly between the different types. By understanding these different categories of love, we can make the connection to how each grouping can lead us to peace.

# Eros

*Eros* is sexual or passionate love, and most akin to the modern construct of romantic love[29]. In Greek myth, it is a form of madness brought about by one of the angel Cupid's arrows. The arrow fissures us and we *fall* in love, as did Paris with Helen, leading to the downfall of Troy and much of the assembled Greek army. In modern times, *eros* has been joined with the broader life force, something akin to a fundamentally blind process of striving for survival and reproduction. Eros love can bring about temporary peace.

# Philia

*Philia*, or friendship, is a shared goodwill form of love that is also the basis for peace. The philosopher Aristotle believed that a person can bear goodwill to another for one of three reasons: that he is useful; that he is pleasant; and above all, that he is good, that is, rational and virtuous. Friendships founded on goodness are associated not only with mutual benefit but also with companionship, dependability, and trust[30]. For Aristotle, the best kind of friendship is that which

---

[29] "These Are the 7 Types of Love | Psychology Today," https://www.psychologytoday.com/us/blog/hide-and-seek/201606/these-are-the-7-types-love.

[30] "Philia – Brotherly Love," The Love Shack, November 29, 2016, https://theloveshack2016.wordpress.com/2016/11/29/philia-aka-brotherly-love/.

lovers have for each other. It is a *philia* born out of *eros*, and that in turn feeds back into *eros* to strengthen and develop love. This is a transforming from a lust for possession into a shared desire for a higher level of understanding of the self, the other, and the world. Real friends seek together to live truer, fuller and more peaceful lives by relating to each other authentically and helping each other in the spirit of a greater love.

## Storge

*Storge* or familial love, pertains to the love between parents and their children, as well as to extended family. This kind of love is born out of familiarity or dependency. It is much less contingent on our personal qualities[31]. There is a wide-ranging maturity and usefulness to familial love as it is not just pleasurable but necessary for survival of the individuals in the family unit. From this kind of unity, true love and attachment develop between the individuals of the family that leads to true peace.

---

[31] Roy Liang, "The 8 Types of Love-According to the Ancient Greeks," Medium (Medium, May 23, 2020), https://allad201314.medium.com/the-8-types-of-love-accoding-to-the-ancient-greeks-97bff653bbfd.

# Agape

*Agape* is universal love, such as the love for strangers, nature, or mystical aspects of life. Unlike familial love, it does not depend on any individual or group affiliation. *Agape* can be said to encompass the modern concept of altruism, defined as unselfish concern for the welfare of others[32]. Recent studies link altruism with a number of benefits related to love. In the short-term, an altruistic act leaves a person with a euphoric feeling, the so-called "helper's high." In the longer term, altruism has been associated with better mental and physical health, and even greater longevity. At a social level, altruism as an expression of Agape love serves cooperative intentions to do with resource-sharing and points the way to universal peace.

# Ludus

*Ludus* is playful or uncommitted love. It can involve activities such as teasing and dancing, or more overt flirting, seducing, and conjugating[33]. The focus of this type of love is on fun with no obligations or consequences attached. *Ludus* relationships are

---

[32] Roy Liang, "The 8 Types of Love-According to the Ancient Greeks," Medium (Medium, May 23, 2020), https://allad201314.medium.com/the-8-types-of-love-accoding-to-the-ancient-greeks-97bff653bbfd.

[33] "These Are the 7 Types of Love | Psychology Today," https://www.psychologytoday.com/us/blog/hide-and-seek/201606/these-are-the-7-types-love.

casual, undemanding, and uncomplicated, but can be very long-lasting. *Ludus* works best when both parties are mature and self-sufficient, and both parties understand how this love can create peace.

# Pragma

*Pragma* is a kind of practical love founded on reason or duty and one's longer-term interests, compatibilities, shared goals, and cooperation. For example, in the days of arranged marriages, *pragma* love was very common. Love that starts off as *eros* or *ludus* may develop into *pragma*, and co-exist peacefully together.

# Philautia

*Philautia* is self-love, which can be either healthy or unhealthy. Unhealthy self-love is practiced by individuals who are narcissistic, self-involved, and not interested in loving others, except for their own purposes. Unhealthy self-love can lead to delusional behavior, injustice, conflict, and enmity. Healthy self-love, on the other hand, is akin to self-esteem, which is the cognitive and honest emotional appraisal of an individual's own worth. Healthy *Philautia* is the matrix through which we think, feel, and act, and reflects on our relation to ourselves, and to others, and to the world. In everyday life, people with healthy self-esteem do not need to inflate their self-worth with externals such as income, status, or notoriety, or lean on alcohol, drugs, or sex to give them self-love, or healthy gratification. We need to love ourselves realistically in order to find inner peace

# Love and Peace

In order to find peace through love, we need to focus both on finding inner peace and social love, as well as promoting peace in the world. This can be hard to do, especially when life is difficult, full of obstacles, and very busy. However, by prioritizing love in ourselves, with our families and neighbors, and the world around us, we can attain real peace and a positive direction in life. Here are some practical ways to move from the theories of love to action. Let's examine the different ways in which love is important to finding peace.

**Peace through love of your skills and abilities**. Look closely at your skills, your life situation, and the world around you. With these in mind, it will help you to know what you power you have within you to do that will be fulfilling, motivating, and will bring you peace.

Peace through love of what you do. For many people, a mixture of financial security and following their dreams is at the core of their motivations. Working in a job that one loves focuses an individual on making a difference in the world while also building financial security, personal fulfillment, and a more peaceful world.

**Peace through love of forgiveness.** A key element of finding peace, as well as being able to focus on love, is embracing forgiveness. Forgiving others, for what they have done to you, to people you love, or to themselves, can release a stored-up love within you. Being able to forgive yourself is a way to foster self-love and will bring you peace.

**Peace through love of yourself.** Part of developing your inner peace through love is valuing all the parts of yourself. This may mean accepting a physical characteristic that you have always disliked, or embracing a personality trait. Identify what your strengths and even your failures. Love through self-acceptance is and important step towards finding inner peace. Then, you can start to changing things for the better.

**Peace through love discipline.** We must develop and love the habits or disciplines that can be done every day to create inner peace and social peace. There are many ways to do this like *taichi*, yoga, meditation, being alone in nature, good eating habits, etc. Peace through a daily discipline that you love will clear your mind, enliven your energy and help you achieve greater peace.

**Peace through loving relationships.** When you develop meaningful relationships love is created and spread from you to other people. These loving and meaningful relationships give you a sense of trust and peace

**Peace through lovingkindness.** Being kind to others people who may be strangers or different than we are helps promoting compassion and peace all around us. This requires that we give up fear of others throughout the world and sometimes even volunteer to help others in need.

**Peace through love of nonviolence.** When we teach and practice nonviolence, we stop hurting others by our words, thoughts and deeds. When we stop hurting others we can feel peace within ourselves and all around us.

**Peace through loving political actions.** When help our leaders by speaking out in a loving way against injustice and suffering, we can help create a happier, more prosperous and peaceful world for all. Humanity is one big family and we should try to love all members of our family so there is worldwide peace too.

## Friendship

What is a friend?
A friend is someone who helps me when I need help,
And who I can help when they need a friend.
A friend is someone with who I can share important stuff.
A friend is someone who shows me how to be a better
person.
A friend is forever!
Wouldn't it be great if we could all be friends?

- Children's story

**Friendship** is a state of enduring affection, esteem, intimacy, and trust between two people. In all cultures, friendships are important relationships throughout a person's life span. Studying friendship is important in understanding and practicing peace between individuals, in families and society and among nations. Friendship is generally characterized by five defining features:

1. Friendship involves a series of interactions between individuals or individuals in groups known to each other.

2. Friendship is recognized by all members of the relationship and is characterized by a bond or tie of reciprocated affection.

3. Friendship is not obligatory; two individuals or individuals in a group choose to form a friendship with each other. Close friendships may have no formal duties or legal obligations to one another, whereas friendships between groups may have stated or contractual obligations to each other.

4. Friendship is typically egalitarian and friends are seen and treated as peers. Unlike parent-child relationships, for instance, each individual in a friendship or in a group has about the same amount of power or authority in the relationship.

5. Friendship is almost always characterized by comradeship and shared values as sources of support and providing opportunities for mutual benefit.

Friendships play an important role in healthy human development and adjustments across the life span. Friendships exist in practically every stage of development, although the form they take varies considerably with age. By studying the various stages of human development through the lens of friendship, we can see analogies in how these patterns are similar to the development of political and national friendships and alliances.

## Childhood

Children themselves tend at first to define friendships in terms of interactions, such as "we play together." Differences between friends and non-friends are particularly evident in social pretend play. Children also begin to incorporate more emotional and affective functions into their friendships. Early friendships are expressed with a positive affect toward each other and foster mutual liking, closeness, and loyalty than non-friends do.

Friendships are not always harmonious, however, and young children may engage in conflict with their friends. In fact, in early childhood, friends tend to engage in more conflict than with non-friends. Yet, friends also expend more effort to resolve conflict and are more successful at such resolution than are non-friends. Conflict resolution is frequently seen as one of the important social skills that young children develop within their earliest friendships.

If we examine the analogy of childhood friendships to new nations, such as were created after World War I and after World War II, we see a mutual attraction based on shared values and ambitions. One example is after World War 2 the European powers released their former Arab colonies who formed united fronts, particularly with the young nations of Jordan, Egypt, Syria, Lebanon and Iraq developing peaceful relations between themselves.

## Middle Childhood

Friendships make up an important aspect of development in middle childhood, when much time is devoted to social play and social interaction skills become increasingly important. School-age children spend a great deal of time interacting with peers and thus are presented with many opportunities for extending the friendship skills they acquired in early childhood. Middle school children tend to form friendships with individuals who are similar to themselves in a variety of dimensions.

Children at this age are developing increasing independence from their parents, and their relationships with friends maybe coupled with the social and cognitive advances. Spending time together with a friend may promote the development of shared intimacy—which frequently takes the form of shared secrets—and becomes a defining feature of friendship for children at this age[34]. Friendships in middle childhood are more stable over time than friendships in early childhood yet typically less so than adolescent or adult friendships.

In the same manner, younger nations that come into a later stage of development up to 15 years from their birth, start to develop more sophisticated and closer ties which lead to greater cooperation and connection. An example of how peace was enhanced by the gradual development of mature connection is the integration of white supremacist South Africa with other young African nations after the change of that nation's leadership.

---

[34] "Etheloproxenos," Encyclopedia Britannica, https://www.britannica.com/topic/etheloproxenos.

# Adolescence

Adolescence marks a critical period in the development of friendships [35] .A variety of factors, such as growth in cognitive capabilities and strivings for increased autonomy from parents, contribute to the formation of close friendships in adolescence. Close friendships involve more affection and intimacy than friendships before adolescence. Although relationships to parents remain important sources of support, adolescents begin to seek more support and advice from friends than do children in early or middle childhood. Adolescents also spend more time with friends with whom they engage in particular sports and other friends with whom they participate in the same school club or activity. Some adolescents form friendships with other-sex individuals to whom they were initially romantically attracted.

Here too, we can make the analogy of nations who are maturing in years and deepening their relations with other 'adolescent' nations increasing the peace between them. An example we can look at here is post-war Japan and South Korea who gradually started to deepen their commercial and cultural relations after their bitter history in the early 20th century, and seeing the benefits of gradual friendship being established.

---

[35] Mahmoud Suhaila Banat, "The Effectiveness of A Group Counseling Program," *Journal for the Education of Gifted* (2020).

## Adulthood

Research on friendship in young adulthood has mostly focused on college students where friendships are focused on social or academic shared interests. Young adults who are not in college but are in the work force tend to focus their friendships in social similarities and oftentimes look more for romantic relationships and social friendships. When individuals enter into marriage, both men and women seem to withdraw from friendships with their focus becoming more on family, parenting, and careers. In older adults, outside of their family activities, friendships among same-age peers becomes increasingly important for the sake of support and companionship.

Among nations, we can note the example of more "adult' and peer relationships is how the US and Mexico have developed more a mature friendship based on their understood mutual needs from their earlier history of war and animosity.

## Maintenance of Friendships

Across individuals of all ages, friendships form, evolve, and sometimes dissolve over time. The length and duration of the various phases of a friendship vary across individuals and circumstances.

The maintenance phase of friendship involves engaging in interactions that serve to sustain the relationship. Friends engage in a variety of behaviors to maintain their relationships such as sharing interests, doing recreational or leisure activities together, and exchanging support and advice. Friends typically have conversations about topics such as family issues, other interpersonal relationships, and daily activities. The frequency of interactions between friends is one central determinant of the success of maintaining a friendship[36]. In other words, friendships are not stationary; interactions are required for maintaining a friendship. Convenience is perhaps the most important determinant of the frequency of interactions between friends. Thus, it is easier to maintain friendships with individuals in close proximity (e.g., neighbors) than with those far away (e.g., long-distance friends)[37].

Once an emotional bond of a certain degree has been established, it is more the quality than the quantity of interactions that determines success in maintaining a friendship. In other words, friends who have a long-standing history and who have established a strong affective connection may not need to interact very frequently to maintain their friendship.

Whereas joint satisfaction in the relationship is part of maintaining friendship, another important component is managing and resolving conflict. Although the amount and intensity of conflict vary across individual friendships, conflicts do arise in most friendships. Because conflict involves self-disclosure and exposing one's own vulnerabilities, successful negotiation of disagreements that arise between friends can actually foster increased trust. Friends can

---

[36] Administrator, "Friendship – Iresearch.net," Psychology, March 16, 2017, https://psychology.iresearchnet.com/developmental-psychology/social-development/friendship/.

[37] Neil J. Salkind, *Encyclopedia of Human Development* (1939).

protect each other and provide support for each other against victimization from other peers.

## Friendship Among Nations for Peaceful Relations

Let us magnify what we now know about the development of individual and group friendships and now relate that knowledge to discuss the importance of national and international friendships. There is a long legacy of contractual friendship agreements and the roles they have played in international relations. We must examine the history of concepts and international political theory to explore the role of friendship in the same context as the general concepts of friendship previously discuss as voluntary contractual agreements between states. This is a perspective that has been neglected in the fairly recent re-emergence of scholarship on friendships in politics and international relations. We must set the stage for peaceful relations between nations by discussing some of the most prevalent discourses around friendship in international relations, in particular the scholarship that explores political friendship as analogous to personal friendship and which focuses on the moral and ethical obligations of friendship. This normative view of friendship has become central to the current political views on friendship especially since the modern period.

There are ethical or naturalistic perspectives on friendship between states within international society that have resulted in a loss of the pragmatic and contractual understanding of friendship which is important to diplomatic practice and world peace. We must recover this understanding of the role of friendship in negotiated political agreements that will demonstrate a serious commitment to diplomatic accords rather than a perception of insincerity or 'lip service.'

We must return to the moral side of international friendships and emphasize a need to revisit the diverse ancient conceptualizations of friendship which were wholly dependent on ethical and peaceful concepts. We must offer perspectives of friendship that relate to how friendship agreements have been used to maintain peace and order within international society. Let us focuses on friendships between governments in from a variety of historical settings. Friendship in politics cannot take a purely theoretical approach if there is a desire for true peace among nations.

Through the individual and group lens which views friendship as a structural relationship between security communities we must admit the lack of scholarship on friendship in international relations is due in large part to the prominence of the realist paradigm in international relations which focuses largely on rival and enemy themes. If we analyze some of the earliest classical sources on friendship we must include the utility of friendship in seeking international peace and discuss the ethical relations that bind diverse people and governments together. There is a distinct relationship to the reasons that bind members of the international political community together based on pragmatism and shared ethical concerns which result in contractual friendship that provides political and legal order within the international community and serves as the foundation and basis for political practices of peace and avoids conflict among the modern political systems.

There is always the challenge of prioritizing virtuous friendship as most important but not treating the other types of friendships as second rate. Friendship of utility has a vital role in holding states and nations together and providing order and peace in society. In the international system friendships of utility have been manifest in alliances and treaties between states that respect one another. Contractual agreements do not use the emotional language of love, peace and friendship but they ought to be conditioned on these universal concepts. Agreements represented a legal type of friendship which could be negotiated even based on unequal concepts and obligations could be breached.

The virtuous form of friendship leads to world peace. Friendship and sociability are inherent in human nature and should be the focus on political relations in international society, rather than fear. Civilized nations that adhere to the laws of the harmony of nature always prevail over those nations that focus on unwholesome behaviors and disharmony. International politics have severe and oftentimes catastrophic consequences if diplomatic practices don't take into consideration friendship with the goal of peace.

## Respect

What is Respect?

Respect is caring for yourself, for others, and for things, both living things.

Respect is caring about other people's minds and bodies, and feelings through our kind actions, and words, and even our thoughts.

> Respect is caring about people, even if they sometimes don't respect us[38], because we know that sometimes people are afraid, or have been hurt, and they want to hurt somebody else to get even. But we still have to try to help those people to understand respect.
>
> Respect is living together, caring for this beautiful earth with all its plants, animals, fish, birds, bugs, with all kinds of boys and girls, with all kinds of people, and yes, maybe even with aliens!
>
> Everybody and everything need respect!
>
> - *Children's Book*

Respect is defined in several ways:

- A feeling of deep admiration for someone or something elicited by their abilities, qualities, or achievements.
- Due regard for the feelings, wishes, rights, or traditions of others[39]
- To admire (someone or something) deeply, as a result of their abilities, qualities, or achievements.
- A positive feeling or action shown towards someone or something considered important or held in high esteem or regard.

---

[38] Etan Boritzer, ***What is Respect?*** (2016).

[39] Arushi Arora, "Some Thoughts on Respect," The Millburn Penpoint, https://millburnpenpoint.com/4645/showcase/some-thoughts-on-respect/.

- A sense of admiration for good or valuable qualities.

Respect begins within oneself and stems from dignity, a basic human right. Dignity comes from a place of value, worthiness, and a sense of self-worth. Similarly, in order to build peaceful relationships between nations, each state must have a sense of pride in its people, culture, history, and achievements that constitute self-respect[40].

Respect allows one to build trusting relationships with others. Those individuals and nations who are respected within the international community are most likely to be able to bring or encourage peace. Showing other people respect is a great way to communicate that you care about them. Respect shows that the individual or the nation is kind and compassionate.

## How to Show Respect

### 1. Listen to Others.

Diplomats and government leaders should show respect by practicing active listening to show their respect to other leaders. Then they can offer assistance, acknowledge their achievements, and empathize with their opinions. We need to watch and be quiet when someone else is talking and spend time thinking about what they're saying. Ask follow-up questions to stay engaged in the conversation. Too often, we wait to talk instead of really

[40] Lt. Col. Amy Thompson Lt. Col. Cleve Sylvester Master Sgt. John Ahern, "Treating Others with Respect Is a Core Value," AUSA, September 6, 2019, https://www.ausa.org/articles/treating-others-respect-core-value.

listening to other people's ideas[41]. Even if one disagrees, one should try to consider the point of view and empathize with it before responding.

**2. Affirm People's Opinions.**

Diplomats and government leaders need to let others know that they matter. They show respect when they are talking to someone by validating the other side's opinions. They can also respect achievements by letting the other side know you see how hard they've worked. When you validate people and their achievements, you show them that you respect their hard work and effort.

**3. Empathize with Different Perspectives.**

Diplomats and governments leaders may not completely understand the other side's viewpoint but they can respect it. If there is disagreement on something, it should not be taken personally. Everyone has a different background, and every side has their own reasons for thinking whatever they think. Even if one side doesn't agree with what is presented, a diplomat or government leader may say respectfully, "I never thought of it that way. What makes you say

---

[41] Camber Hill, "12 Ways to Show Respect," WikiHow, September 20, 2022, https://www.wikihow.com/Show-Respect.

that?" Then, they can learn more about the person and their perspective[42].

**4. Disagree Respectfully.**

Diplomats and government leaders should not insult any opinions or ideas if they disagree with them. Instead, they can show respect by acknowledging the common ground before sharing their side. It is necessary to be specific with a critique and avoid any personal insults. Diplomats and government leaders may say politely, "That's a good point. I think I'm seeing it a little differently though..."

**5. Apologize When Wrong.**

It shows a great deal of maturity and respect for diplomats and government leaders if they make a mistake to say simply, "I'm sorry." It is not necessary to make excuses but one can own up to what they did. It might also be helpful to have a plan in place so mistakes don't happen again.

**6. Call Out Disrespectful Behavior.**

It's OK to let the people around you know that you won't tolerate disrespectful behavior. If someone is being rude or disrespectful to someone else, we can pull them aside and ask them about their

---

[42] "Take Online Courses. Earn College Credit. Research Schools, Degrees & Careers," Study.com | Take Online Courses. Earn College Credit. Research Schools, Degrees & Careers, https://study.com/academy/lesson/realistic-vs-optimistic-thinking.html.

behavior. Try to explain that what the other party did was wrong and how there are better ways to resolve any conflict.

7. **Show Gratitude.**

It's important for diplomats and government leaders to show respect by thanking other nations for their assistance and their support when they have helped that nation through tough times or been there for the long run. Gratitude is a compliment and others will want to help that nation again.

8. **Compliment the Achievements of Others.**

   Diplomats and government leaders can highlight when people around do well in their jobs. They show respect by drawing attention to achievements and celebrating them. Keeping a positive attitude toward others will focus attention on the continuation of goodwill, cooperation, and peace.

9. **Follow Through on Commitments.**

Diplomats and government leaders show respect by sticking with their commitments and treaties with other nations. Being reliable shows respect for shows that one is making a special effort to be compliant with agreements. Respecting other people's efforts and time is important to creating trust and peace.

**Help Others.**

If a friend is struggling, lend them a helping hand. This is the human action to take and shows respect for another person or nation's survival. If there is stability and peace with your neighbor or another friendly nation that can be demonstrated by helping them, that is a great statement of respect[43].

**10. Taking Care of One's Own.**

Diplomats and government leaders should give their citizens the same respect and care they give themselves by building a good national support system. Self-destructive behaviors by diplomats and government leaders must be avoided or there will be no respect or peace within the land. Treat all citizens with equal kindness and respect.

**Summary**

By following these simple and logical steps to real respect, we can achieve real peace. Without respecting ourselves and others, there will always be conflict between individuals and nations. Peace based on fear is not long-lasting. Real peace is based on the real understanding between individuals and nations that begins with simple respect and can transform even to friendship and love.

---

[43] Camber Hill, "12 Ways to Show Respect," WikiHow, https://www.wikihow.com/Show-Respect.

## Bibliography

Administrator. “Friendship – Iresearch,net.” Psychology, March 16, 2017. https://psychology.iresearchnet.com/developmental-psychology/social-development/friendship/.

Arora, Arushi. “Some Thoughts on Respect.” The Millburn Penpoint. Accessed October 25, 2022. https://millburnpenpoint.com/4645/showcase/some-thoughts-on-respect/.

Banat, Mahmoud Suhaila. “The Effectiveness of A Group Counseling Program.” *Journal for the Education of Gifted* (2020).

Boritzer, Etan. *What Is Respect?*. 2016.

“Etheloproxenos.” Encyclopedia Britannica https://www.britannica.com/topic/etheloproxenos.

Hill, Camber. “12 Ways to Show Respect.” WikiHow, September 20, 2022. https://www.wikihow.com/Show-Respect.

Liang, Roy. “The 8 Types of Love-According to the Ancient Greeks.” Medium. Medium, May 23, 2020. https://allad201314.medium.com/the-8-types-of-love-accoding-to-the-ancient-greeks-97bff653bbfd.

Lt. Col. Amy Thompson Lt. Col. Cleve Sylvester Master Sgt. John Ahern. “Treating Others with Respect Is a Core Value.” AUSA, September 6, 2019. https://www.ausa.org/articles/treating-others-respect-core-value.

"Philia – Brotherly Love." The Love Shack, November 29, 2016. https://theloveshack2016.wordpress.com/2016/11/29/philia-aka-brotherly-love/.

Salkind, Neil J. *Encyclopedia of Human Development.* 1939.

"Take Online Courses. Earn College Credit. Research Schools, Degrees & Careers." Study.com | Take Online Courses. Earn College Credit. Research Schools, Degrees & Careers. https://study.com/academy/lesson/realistic-vs-optimistic-thinking.html.

"These Are the 7 Types of Love | Psychology Today." https://www.psychologytoday.com/us/blog/hide-and-seek/201606/these-are-the-7-types-love.

# Chapter 3

# Pax Americana

When we approach the subject of peace in terms of the American experience, we must also discuss peace in relative terms of anthropological, political, and historical realities. Is man peaceful by nature? It would seem that Charles Darwin's theories of the 'Survival of Species' intimate the competitive and aggressive nature of living things, including mammals and man. Only the strongest survive is Darwin's philosophical thrust, although later naturalists pointed out that societies of insects, plants, rodents, and other earth creatures survived through cooperative efforts. However, if we accept man's endemic aggressive violent, and often deadly nature, we can then ask if the ends—survival, and propagation of the species—justify the means, aggression, and violence. This is an age-old philosophical and moral question: Does the end justify the means? Or stated more pointedly for this critical analysis: Is war a means to peace? As to the question of American militarism and power, as examined in relation to its stated means toward a peaceful and just global society, the answers must be scrutinized carefully.

As we have already studied various aspects of peace, let us now briefly look at the nature of war. War is generally defined as a violent conflict between states or nations. Nations go to war for a variety of reasons. It has been argued that a nation will go to war if the benefits of war are deemed to outweigh the disadvantages and if there is a sense that there is not another mutually agreeable solution. Let us examine more closely the general reasons for war.

## Reasons for War[44]

1. **Economic Gain**

Often wars are caused by one country's wish to take control of another country's wealth. Whatever the other reasons for war may be, there is very often an economic motive underlying most conflicts, even if the stated aim of the war is presented to the public as something nobler.

In pre-industrial times, the gains desired by a warring country might be precious materials such as gold and silver or livestock such as cattle and horses. In modern times, the resources hoped to be gained from war take the form of things like oil, minerals, or materials used in manufacturing.

Some scientists believe that as the world's population increases and basic resources become scarce, wars will often be fought over fundamental essentials, such as water and food.

---

[44] Paul Goodman, "The 8 Main Reasons for War," Owlcation (Owlcation, October 6, 2014), https://owlcation.com/social-sciences/The-Main-Reasons-For-War.

### 2. Territorial Gain

A country might decide that it needs more land, either for living space, agricultural use, or other purposes. Territory can also be used as "buffer zones" between two hostile enemies.

Related to buffer zones are proxy wars. These are conflicts that are fought indirectly between opposing powers in a third country. Each power supports the side which best suits its logistical, military, and economic interests. Proxy wars were widespread during the Cold War.

### 3. Religion

Religious conflicts often have very deep roots. They can lie dormant for decades, only to re-emerge in a flash at a later date.

Religious wars can often be tied to other reasons for conflict, such as nationalism or revenge for a perceived historical slight in the past.

While different religions fighting against each other can be a cause of war, different sects within a religion (for example, Protestant and Catholic, or Sunni and Shiite) battling against one another can also instigate war.

### 4. Nationalism

Nationalism, in this context, essentially means attempting to prove that your country is superior to another by violent subjugation. This often takes the form of an invasion.

Dr. Richard Ned Lebow, Professor of International Political Theory at the Department of War Studies, Kings College London, contends that while other causes of war may be present, nationalism, or spirit, is nearly always a factor. He writes:

"Literature on war and its causes assumes security is the principal motive of states and insecurity the major cause of war. Following Plato and Aristotle, I posit spirit as the fundamental drive with distinct goals for war. There can be little doubt that the spirit is the principal cause of war across the centuries."

Related to nationalism is imperialism, which is built on the idea that conquering other countries is glorious and brings honor and esteem to the conqueror.

**5. Revenge**

Seeking to punish, redress a grievance, or simply strike back for a perceived slight can often be a factor in war. Revenge also relates to nationalism, as the people of a country which has been wronged are motivated to fight back by pride and spirit.

Unfortunately, this can lead to an endless chain of retaliatory wars being set in motion, which is very difficult to stop. Any distinction between the victim and aggressor can often become blurred, with all participants perceiving themselves as fighting a just war to right historical wrongs. Historically, revenge has been a factor in many European wars.

## 6. Civil War

These generally take place when there is sharp internal disagreement within a country. The disagreement can be about who rules, how the country should be run or the people's rights. These internal rifts often turn into chasms that result in violent conflict between two or more opposing groups.

Civil wars can also be sparked by separatist groups who want to form their own independent country or, as in the case of the American Civil War, states wanting to secede from a larger union.

## 7. Revolutionary War

These occur when a large section of the population of a country revolts against the individual or group that rules the country because they are dissatisfied with their leadership.

Revolutions can begin for various reasons, including economic hardship amongst certain sections of the population or perceived injustices committed by the ruling group. Other factors can contribute, too, such as unpopular wars with other countries. Revolutionary wars can quickly descend into civil wars.

## 8. Defensive War

In the modern world, where military aggression is more widely questioned, countries will often argue that they are fighting in a purely defensive capacity against an aggressor or potential aggressor and that their war is, therefore, a "just" war.

These defensive wars can be especially controversial when they are launched preemptively; the argument is that: "We are attacking them before they inevitably attack us."

## What is Pax Americana?

Is America militaristic or peaceful? In studying the concept of peace and war, we can now more closely study America, with its vast war-making resources versus its historical ideals of freedom and justice. To understand the overwhelming military, industrial, scientific and cultural worldwide influence of the United States from the beginning of the 20th century to our current times, it is necessary to understand how and why America's dominance came into existence. As we study both the positive and negative effects of this 120-year historical phenomenon, we can begin to make judgments on the utilities and outcomes of this complex issue. How can we judge the results of the expansion and maintenance of the power, wealth influence, and war-making abilities of the United States? One useful way is to study the commonly accepted principle that the overwhelming force and presence of the United States in world affairs has resulted in a purported sustained period of peace and prosperity globally, the so-called period of Pax Americana.

*Pax Americana* (Latin for "American Peace," modeled after *Pax Romana* and *Pax Britannica*) is a term applied to the concept of relative peace in the Western Hemisphere and later throughout the world in the period after the end of World War II in 1945 when the United States emerged the world's dominant economic and military power. In this sense, *Pax Americana* has come to describe the military and financial position of the United States relative to other nations. For example, the Marshall Plan, for which the United States spent an unprecedented USD $13 billion (in today's value: USD 2.139 Trillion) after World War II to rebuild the economies of Western Europe, has been described as the launching of the Pax Americana.[45]

It is useful, however, to go further back even to the roots of the American Revolution and the founding of the Republic in 1789 to understand the conflicting views of America as a nation and people of great and idealistic aspirations for freedom, prosperity, and peace, as contrasted to America's evident militarism and penchant for violence and dominance.

If we review the *American Declaration of Independence* (1776), we find only one mention of peace:

> *He has kept among us, in times of peace, Standing Armies without the Consent of our legislatures. He has affected to render the Military independent of and superior to the Civil power.*

This is, of course, a reference to the ruling British monarch of the time, King George III, and not to any principle or course of action that the 13 colonies propose to institute.

---

[45] "Pax Americana," Wikipedia (Wikimedia Foundation, October 23, 2022), https://en.wikipedia.org/wiki/Pax_Americana.

In the *American Constitution* (1787), the First Amendment has the word peace in it, though used as an adverb, not a noun.

> *Congress shall make no law respecting an establishment of religion or prohibiting the free exercise thereof; or abridging the freedom of speech, or of the press; or the right of the people peaceably to assemble, and to petition the Government for a redress of grievances.*

Here too, the word peace is not used as a noun to state a goal but refers to a description of the people's right to gather in that manner.

The Third Amendment is the only other place in the Constitution with the word peace in it, though also not used to state a goal of the American people.

> *No Soldier shall, in time of peace be quartered in any house, without the consent of the Owner, nor in time of war, but in a manner to be prescribed by law.*

Some political anthropologists even point out a certain DNA in the American psyche born of the primarily British-American 'Fathers of the Republic.' The American colonists and their forefathers were part of the Age of the Conquest beginning in the 15th century when exploration of the globe by the English, the Spanish and Portuguese, the French, the Dutch, the Belgians, and other European countries resulted in the genocide of native peoples in the Americas, Africa, and Asia, as well as the enslavement, torture, and exploitation of these peoples and races for the greedy enrichment of the European nations. It can even be argued that the White tribes of Europe have caused more death and destruction historically than any other race or people on the planet through their sheer rapaciousness, their ingenious scientific methods of war, and their unrelenting penchant for war among themselves and perhaps more importantly for this examination, the conquest of Black, Yellow, Brown, and Red-skinned peoples within and outside their borders. The American people, from the earliest European White invaders of the American continents to the settlers of the Americas, brought this endemic penchant for violence, greed, and militarism with them wherever they went, as recorded even from the earliest Greek and Roman transnational empires to the Crusades and the just-referred imperialist era.

### The Beginnings of American Militarism

After its victory in the Spanish–American War of 1898 and the subsequent acquisition of Cuba, Puerto Rico, the Philippines, and Guam, the United States gained a colonial empire. By ejecting Spain from the Americas, the United States shifted its position to an uncontested regional power, and extended its influence into Southeast Asia and Oceania. Although U.S. capital investments within the Philippines and Puerto Rico were relatively small, these colonies were strategic outposts for expanding trade with Latin America and Asia, particularly China.

In the Caribbean area, the United States established a sphere of influence in line with the Monroe Doctrine, which prohibited any foreign military activities in the Caribbean Sea. The events around the start of the 20th century demonstrated that the United States undertook an obligation to impose a Pax Americana. As in similar instances elsewhere, this Pax Americana was not quite clearly marked in its geographical limit, nor was it guided by any theoretical consistency, but rather by the merits of the case and the test of immediate expediency in each to permit any European power to interfere in Americas, the Monroe Doctrine was indirectly aided by the Royal Navy. British commercial interests in South America, which comprised a valuable component of the informal empire that accompanied Britain's overseas possessions, and the economic importance of the United States as a trading partner, ensured that intervention by Britain's rival European powers could not engage with the Americas.

## Early United States Military Interventions

Prior to the modern era, the United States was continuously in international wars after the American Revolution against the British. There were major conflicts from the War of 1812 again against the British, the continuous wars against the Native American nations during the entire $19^{th}$ century, the Mexican-American War (1848), and the American Civil War fought from 1861 to 1865.

As we have said, if we begin to study the term Pax America and what the actual historical ramifications of this concept were and still are, we can see how this term is really more of an idealistic principle than demonstrated in actual historical facts. We will soon examine in more detail how this period has also proved to be a period of American-induced wars and human catastrophes. But first, let us examine America's numerous militaristic roles in world events even prior to the post-World War II period termed Pax Americana to understand the growth of American militarism.

## The War of 1812

The American colonies had won their independence from Great Britain in 1783. The War of 1812 was the first foreign war that the American nation and people undertook, and it is worth studying this war to witness the historical beginnings of American militarism. The War of 1812 was a byproduct of the broader conflict between Great Britain and France over who would dominate Europe and the wider world. Our question of American militarism is traditionally viewed historically as a necessity for the survival of United States commerce, but the war aims of the United States were more complex and escalated the United States into the leading ranks of powerful global military armies.

The United States had many reasons for going to war in 1812: Britain's interference with its trade and impressment of its seamen; Americans' desire to expand settlement into Indian, British, and Spanish territories; aspirations to conquer Canada and end British influence in North America; and upholding the nation's sovereignty and vindicating its honor.

In Britain's effort to control the world's oceans, the British Royal Navy encroached upon American maritime rights and cut into American trade during the Napoleonic Wars. In response, the young

American republic declared war on Britain on June 18, 1812. The two leading causes of the war were the British Orders-in-Council, which limited American trade with Europe, and impressment, the Royal Navy's practice of taking seamen from American merchant vessels to fill out the crews of its own chronically undermanned warships. Under the authority of the Orders in Council, the British seized some 400 American merchant ships and their cargoes between 1807 and 1812. Press gangs, though ostensibly targeting British subjects for naval service, also swept up 6,000 to 9,000 Americans into the crews of British ships between 1803 and 1812. Some of the impressed sailors were born in British possessions but had migrated to the United States. In contrast, many others had attained citizenship that was either in question or simply could not be documented.

American armies invaded British Canada in 1812 but had little real success against the superior British land and sea forces. By 1814, the United States was thrown on the defensive because the defeat of Napoleon Bonaparte in Europe enabled the British to shift additional resources to the war in America. The British took the offensive and even occupied Washington, DC, burning the public buildings there. Note that the British burned the President's mansion at 1600 Pennsylvania Avenue, and after the war ended, it was repainted white, and from then on, it has been known as the White House.

The war went worse for the Americans. American privateers also took a toll on British shipping early in the war, but the British used their superior navy to ship more troops to Canada, to keep them supplied, and to blockade and raid the American coast. The blockade had a devastating impact on the U.S. economy and public finance, and also kept most American warships in port. However, the Americans kept fighting and won victories.

Ultimately, the War of 1812 ended in a draw on the battlefield, and the peace treaty reflected this. The Treaty of Ghent was signed on December 24, 1814. This agreement provided for returning to the *status quo ante bellum*, which meant that the antagonists agreed to return to the state that had existed before the war and restore all conquered territory.

Both sides could claim victory, the British because they held on to Canada and their maritime rights, and the United States because just fighting the “Conqueror of Napoleon” and the “Mistress of the Seas” to a draw vindicated its sovereignty and earned the respect of Europe. As British diplomat Augustus J. Foster acknowledged at the war’s end, “The Americans . . . have brought us to speak of them with respect.”

The only real losers in the war were the indigenous nations of North America, who were defeated in two wars connected to the War of 1812: Tecumseh’s War in the Old Northwest and the Creek War in the Old Southwest. American success in these wars opened the door for westward expansion and threatened the indigenous peoples and their ways of life east of the Mississippi River.

The war laid the foundations for the emergence of Canada as an independent nation and induced the British to seek peaceful relations with the United States for the remainder of the 19th century and beyond. It also helped forge the United States into a nation. Americans could celebrate their victories on the high seas and land. America had emerged as a world power.

## The Spanish-American War[46]

The Spanish-American War was an 1898 conflict between the United States and Spain that ended Spanish colonial rule in the Americas and resulted in the U.S. acquiring territories in the western Pacific and Latin America.

The war originated in the Cuban struggle for independence from Spain, which began in February 1895. Spain's brutally repressive measures to halt the rebellion were graphically portrayed for the U.S. public by several sensational newspapers engaging in *yellow journalism*, the term coined in the 19th century to describe journalism that relies on eye-catching headlines, exaggeration, and sensationalism to increase sales ("fake news" today).

American sympathy for the Cuban rebels rose. The growing popular demand for U.S. intervention became an insistent chorus after the still-unexplained sinking in Havana harbor of the American battleship *USS Maine*, which had been sent to protect U.S. citizens and property after anti-Spanish rioting in Havana.

---

[46] "War of 1812 Overview," USS Constitution Museum, March 19, 2019, https://ussconstitutionmuseum.org/major-events/war-of-1812-overview/.

Was the sinking of the *USS Maine* battleship a false flag attack? There are theories that an American sabotage plot by different interested parties to start a war against the Spaniards postulated that a bomb was planted on the inside by a Navy person and the other a bomb planted on the outside of the ship by an unknown saboteur. A 1976 investigation by the US Navy concluded that the explosion happened because of a fire on board and that no mine or explosive was used. However, the conspiracy theories continue to speculate that the U.S. government needed a reason to start a war to gain Spanish Cuba, Puerto Rico, the Philippines, and Guam.

Spain announced an armistice on April 9 and speeded up its new program to grant Cuba limited powers of self-government. But the U.S. Congress soon afterward issued resolutions that declared Cuba's right to independence, demanded the withdrawal of Spain's armed forces from the island, and authorized the use of force by President William McKinley to secure that withdrawal while renouncing any U.S. design for annexing Cuba.

Spain declared war on the United States on April 24, followed by a U.S. declaration of war on the 25th, which was made retroactive to April 21. The ensuing war was pathetically one-sided since Spain had readied neither its army nor its navy for a distant war with the formidable power of the United States.

In the early morning hours of May 1, 1898, Commodore George Dewey led a U.S. naval squadron into Manila Bay in the Philippines. He destroyed the anchored Spanish fleet in two hours before pausing the Battle of Manila Bay to order his crew a second breakfast. In total, fewer than 10 American seamen were lost, while Spanish losses were estimated at over 370. Manila itself was occupied by U.S. troops by August.

The elusive Spanish Caribbean fleet under Adm. Pascual Cervera was located in Santiago harbor in Cuba by U.S. reconnaissance. An army of regular troops and volunteers under Gen. William Shafter (including then-former assistant secretary of the Navy Theodore Roosevelt and his 1st Volunteer Cavalry, the "Rough Riders") landed on the coast east of Santiago and slowly advanced on the city to force Cervera's fleet out of the harbor.

Cervera led his squadron out of Santiago on July 3 and tried to escape westward along the coast. In the ensuing battle, all of his ships came under heavy fire from U.S. guns and were beached in a burning or sinking condition. Santiago surrendered to Shafter on July 17, thus effectively ending the brief but momentous war.

*The Treaty of Paris* ending the Spanish-American War was signed on December 10, 1898. In it, Spain renounced all claims to Cuba, ceded Guam and Puerto Rico to the United States, and transferred sovereignty over the Philippines to the United States for $20 million.

The Spanish-American War was an important turning point in the history of both antagonists. Spain's defeat decisively turned the nation's attention away from its overseas colonial adventures and inward upon its domestic needs, a process that led to both a cultural and a literary renaissance and two decades of much-needed economic development in Spain.

The victorious United States, on the other hand, emerged from the war as a world military power with far-flung overseas possessions and a new stake in international politics that would soon lead it to play a determining role in the affairs of Europe and the rest of the world.

## The Philippine-American War

On February 4, 1899, just two days before the U.S. Senate ratified the treaty, fighting broke out between American forces and Filipino nationalists led by Emilio Aguinaldo, who sought independence rather than a change in colonial rulers. Philippine insurgents who had fought against Spanish rule soon turned their guns against their new American occupiers. The Philippine-American War began in February of 1899 and lasted until 1902. Ten times more U.S. troops died suppressing revolts in the Philippines than in defeating Spain. The ensuing Philippine-American War lasted three years.

The decision by U.S. policymakers to annex the Philippines was not without domestic controversy. Americans who advocated annexation evinced a variety of motivations: desire for commercial opportunities in Asia, concern that the Filipinos were incapable of self-rule, and fear that if the United States did not take control of the islands, another power (such as Germany or Japan) might do so. Meanwhile, American opposition to U.S. colonial rule of the Philippines came in many forms, ranging from those who thought it morally wrong for the United States to be engaged in colonialism to those who feared that annexation might eventually permit the non-white Filipinos to have a role in the American national government. Others were wholly unconcerned about the moral or racial implications of imperialism and sought only to oppose the policies of President William McKinley's administration.

After the Spanish-American War, while the American public and politicians debated the annexation question, Filipino revolutionaries under Aguinaldo seized control of most of the Philippines' main island of Luzon. They proclaimed the establishment of the independent Philippine Republic. When it became clear that U.S. forces were intent on imposing American colonial control over the islands, the early clashes between the two sides in 1899 swelled into an all-out war. Americans tended to refer to the ensuing conflict as an "insurrection" rather than acknowledge the Filipinos' contention that they were fighting to ward off a foreign invader.

There were two phases to the Philippine-American War. From February to November of 1899, the first phase was dominated by Aguinaldo's ill-fated attempts to fight a conventional war against the better-trained and equipped American troops. The second phase was marked by the Filipinos' shift to guerrilla-style warfare. It began in November of 1899 and lasted through the capture of Aguinaldo in 1901 and into the spring of 1902, when most organized Filipino resistance had dissipated. President Theodore Roosevelt proclaimed a general amnesty and declared the conflict over on July 4, 1902, although minor uprisings and insurrections against American rule periodically occurred in the following years.

The war was brutal on both sides. U.S. forces at times burned villages, implemented civilian concentration camp policies, and employed torture on suspected guerrillas, while Filipino fighters also tortured captured soldiers and terrorized civilians who cooperated with American forces. Many civilians died during the conflict due to the fighting, cholera and malaria epidemics, and food shortages caused by several agricultural catastrophes.

Even as the fighting went on, the colonial government that the United States established in the Philippines in 1900 under future President William Howard Taft launched a pacification campaign that became known as the "policy of attraction." Designed to win over key elites and other Filipinos who did not embrace Aguinaldo's plans for the Philippines, this policy permitted a significant degree of self-government, introduced social reforms, and implemented plans for economic development. Over time, this program gained important Filipino adherents and undermined the revolutionaries' popular appeal, significantly aiding the United States military effort to win the war.[47]

By 1900, the United States possessed the world's largest industrial capacity and national income, surpassing the United Kingdom and Germany. The United States lost its Pacific and regionally bounded nature towards the end of the 19th century. The government adopted protectionism after the Spanish–American War and built up the navy, the "Great White Fleet," to expand the reach of U.S. power. When Theodore Roosevelt became President in 1901, he accelerated a foreign policy shift away from isolationism toward

[47] U.S. Department of State, https://history.state.gov/milestones/1899-1913/war.

foreign intervention, which had begun under his predecessor, William McKinley.

## Gunboat Diplomacy

President Theodore Roosevelt is often credited with expanding America's use of gunboat diplomacy. Roosevelt famously said that his diplomatic motto was to “speak softly and carry a big stick,” which, he said, meant that the nation had to be ready to back up words with force.

The practice of backing up diplomatic efforts with a visible show of military might. A nation using gunboat diplomacy uses implicit military threats to achieve its policy objectives.

A gunboat was a relatively small ship that could navigate through shallow waters; easy to maneuver, the boats were fitted with heavy weapons.

The most obvious examples of gunboat diplomacy come from the 19th and early 20th centuries. In 1854, Japan and the United States signed the Treaty of Kanagawa, opening up trade between the two nations for the first time in 200 years. The agreement came about after Commodore Matthew Perry led a naval squadron to Tokyo Bay. As the US State Department has put it, “Perry arrived in Japanese waters with a small squadron of U.S. Navy ships, because he and others believed the only way to convince the Japanese to accept western trade was to display a willingness to use its advanced firepower.”

Roosevelt built up the US military might and routinely made a practice of showing off the nation's might as a way to pre-empt potential challenges. To show off America's naval power, Roosevelt sent a naval fleet worldwide on a tour that lasted 14 months. The fleet was known as the Great White Fleet (its ships were painted white instead of the usual gray) and consisted of 16 battleships manned by 14,000 sailors. The fleet set out on December 16, 1907 and concluded its journey on February 22, 1909. The Great White Fleet called in Hawaii, New Zealand, Australia, Japan, and Egypt, before continuing to Italy and Gibraltar. (Along the way, the sailors provided assistance to victims of an earthquake in Sicily.)

In theory, the era of gunboat diplomacy ended with Franklin Roosevelt's first term. FDR announced his "good neighbor" policy in his first inaugural address, vowing that "in the field of world policy, I would dedicate this nation to the policy of the good neighbor—the neighbor who resolutely respects himself and, because he does so, respects the rights of others."

## American Imperialist Expansionism into Latin America[48]

The U.S. victory over Spain in 1898 commenced a tremendous expansion of U.S. power and influence in Latin America, especially

48 "United States–Latin American Relations," Encyclopedia.com, https://www.encyclopedia.com/humanities/encyclopedias-almanacs-transcripts-and-maps/united-states-latin-american-relations.

in the Caribbean. In 1902 U.S. forces departed Cuba but left in their wake an independent republic beholden to the United States and, by terms of the Platt Amendment, subject to U.S. intervention. U.S. interests in a canal across the Isthmus of Panama increased. When the Nicaraguan leader José Santos Zelaya refused to yield sovereign rights over a passage across Nicaragua, President Theodore Roosevelt (1901–1909), who favored the route across Panama, turned his attention to the negotiation of a canal treaty with Colombia.

The terms ran afoul of Colombian nationalist sentiment. The U.S. government threw its military and economic support to a successful revolutionary movement by Panamanian dissidents and forced the signing of a canal treaty with Panama.

In the 1902–1903 Venezuelan debt crisis, in which Germany, Great Britain, and Italy blockaded the Venezuelan coast, Roosevelt voiced concern over European intervention in the hemisphere. He used the Venezuelan debt imbroglio as justification to meddle in the debt-plagued Dominican Republic and announced the Roosevelt Corollary to the Monroe Doctrine, whereby the United States upheld the doctrine by intervening in Latin America to "prevent European intervention." Citing the persistent unrest in Cuba, Roosevelt dispatched an army to the island in October 1906. For three years, Americans ruled Cuba.

In Central America, the United States supported the isthmian peace treaties of 1907, and Roosevelt's successor, William Howard Taft (1909–1913), pushed U.S. financial intrusion, known as dollar diplomacy, as the means of avoiding the use of troops. Dollar diplomacy presumably offered the United States yet another means of asserting its own variation of "enlightened" administration over unruly and warring governments. The approach rarely worked, however. In 1912 Taft dispatched a military force to Nicaragua, and a U.S. military presence remained in that country until 1925.

President Woodrow Wilson (1913–1921) condemned "gunboat diplomacy" and dollar diplomacy as imperialism, but his determination to advance U.S. economic interests, preserve U.S. security interests in the face of German operations in the region, and especially to "teach" Latins to "elect good men" transformed him into the biggest interventionist of all U.S. leaders. Though pledging to seek no territorial concessions from Latin American republics, Wilson tried to influence the course of the Mexican Revolution (1910–1917), dispatched an occupying force to Veracruz in April 1914, and, following the raid by the revolutionary Pancho Villa on Columbus, New Mexico, in 1916, sent the Pershing Expedition deep into northern Mexico. In 1915 the Wilson administration launched a nineteen-year de facto military occupation of Haiti and, in 1916 established eight-year military governance of the Dominican Republic.

U.S. involvement in World War I brought an expansion of U.S. political, and especially economic, involvement throughout Latin America. Latin American intellectual and literary figures decried the North American cultural threat to Latin traditions. The United States emerged in the 1920s as the overwhelmingly dominant economic presence in Latin America and, relying on its economic strength, began to dismantle its empire in the Caribbean, send financial advisers to Latin America, and negotiate more positively with Mexico in petroleum disputes brought on by the Mexican constitution of 1917. In late 1926 the United States commenced a large-scale intervention in Nicaragua against the guerrilla army of Augusto César Sandino that lasted until 1933, when U.S. forces had been largely supplanted by the Nicaraguan National Guard under Anastasio Somoza García.

## America in World War I

### How the War Began

For decades, tensions had been growing between the nations of Europe. In the summer of 1914, the heir to the throne of Austria-Hungary was assassinated, setting off a sequence of events that eventually drew most of Europe into full-scale war. The Central Powers (led by Germany, Austria-Hungary, and the Ottoman Empire) fought the Allies (led by France, Great Britain, and Russia) as the conflict spread from Europe to the Middle East and then to other parts of the world.

### U.S. Neutrality

The United States remained neutral at the beginning of the war. Individual Americans supported one side or the other, although the majority were sympathetic to the Allies. Many contributed to relief efforts; others volunteered as ambulance drivers or nurses, or even as pilots and soldiers. However, most agreed with President Woodrow Wilson's commitment to keeping the U.S. out of the fighting.

Overseas, the war continued through 1915 and 1916. On the Western Front (in France and Belgium), the fighting bogged down into trench warfare, with combatants on both sides living and dying below ground in squalid, filthy conditions. Most of the other battlefronts also remained deadlocked. The opposing armies threw millions of men at each other in massive battles, and technological advances provided new ways of inflicting death and damage, but neither side could gain the upper hand.

Some Americans felt that their country had a duty to step in to stop the slaughter, but most believed that the pointless carnage proved that the U.S. had been right to stay out of the war.

**America Enters the War**[49]

On the afternoon of May 7, 1915, the British ocean liner *Lusitania* was torpedoed without warning by a German submarine off the south coast of Ireland. Within 20 minutes, the vessel sank into the Celtic Sea. Of 1,959 passengers and crew, 1,198 people drowned, including 128 Americans.

In early 1917, a series of events changed American attitudes. After the *Lusitania* sinking, Germany had prohibited its submarines from sinking civilian and neutral ships, due largely to U.S. protests. In February 1917, it resumed unrestricted submarine warfare against all ships in the war zone. Shortly afterward, an intercepted German

---

[49] "The U.S. in WWI - Overview," Home - World War I Centennial, https://www.worldwar1centennial.org/index.php/edu-home/edu-topics/579-overview-general-collections/4989-the-u-s-in-wwi-overview.html.

telegram revealed a plan offering Mexico territory it had lost to the U.S. during the Mexican-American War (1846-48) in exchange for its support in the war. On April 6, 1917, the United States of America officially entered World War I on the Allies' side. Over the next year and a half, millions of Americans served overseas and supported the nation's war effort at home.

The U.S. government took an active role in mobilizing American industry and society in support of the war effort. In France, General John “Black Jack” Pershing led the effort to organize millions of incoming American troops into an effective fighting force. Meanwhile, German successes on other battlefronts allowed them to focus their efforts on the Western Front.

**Winning the War**

In the spring of 1918, the Germans launched a major series of attacks, finally breaking the stalemate and advancing all along the Western Front. U.S. forces were thrown into action and helped turn back the German assault. Over the summer and into the fall of 1918, the Americans played an emerging role as the Allies finally pushed back the Germans on the Western Front. The Allies also advanced on other battlefronts. One by one, the Central Powers surrendered until Germany stood alone. Finally, on the morning of November 11, 1918, Germany signed an armistice that brought the fighting to an end.

**Peace and Aftermath**

Against the massive backdrop of loss and suffering, the world nations came together in Paris to negotiate the post-war peace treaties. People around the globe hoped that the peace conference would lead to a new era of justice and cooperation. Unfortunately, the resulting Treaty of Versailles and its related agreements failed to capture this spirit and in fact, planted the seeds of World War II and other future conflicts by humiliating and further punishing the Germans and by creating official national mandates for the victors in the Middle East. The Allies cut up the surrendered Ottoman Empire into countries that had existed in biblical times, such as Lebanon, Syria, Palestine, Iraq, Jordan, and the North African countries of Egypt, Tunisia, Libya, Algeria, and Morocco. These newly formed countries were placed under victorious European rule—particularly the British and French—to exploit these countries' wealth, especially their oil, gas, and mineral deposits.

### Legacy

World War I marked the end of the old European order and the beginning of an era that would be dominated by other forces, including the eventual rise of the United States as a global power. The mobilization of the U.S. economy and society and the service and sacrifice of millions of Americans helped end the war and laid the foundation for the emergence of the U.S. as a world superpower later in the 20th Century. For most Americans, going to war in 1917 was about removing the German threat to the U.S. homeland," says Michael S. Neiberg, professor of history at the U.S. Army War College. "But after the war, President Wilson developed a much more expansive vision to redeem the sin of war by founding a new world order, which created controversy and bitterness in the United States."

## The League of Nations

The burden of sending men off to die weighed on Wilson's conscience. It was one reason why he proposed the creation of the League of Nations, an international body based on collective security. But joining the League required the United States to sacrifice a measure of sovereignty. When judged against the butcher's bill of this war, Wilson thought it was a small price to pay. Others, like Wilson's longtime nemesis Senator Henry Cabot Lodge, believed that the United States should be free to pursue its own interests and not be beholden to an international body. America hadn't fought a war only to relinquish its newfound stature as a military power.

As soldiers returned home and the victory parades faded, the fight over the League of Nations turned bitter. The American Congress voted against joining the league despite President Wilson's argument for the U.S.'s joining it. Here is the first example of a great American leader who actively sought global peace but was not supported by most of the American people nor the majority of the legislative U.S. Congress. This rejection of America's role in international peacekeeping efforts led to the American political movement of 'Isolationism' up to the first years of World War II.

Isolationists advocated non-involvement in European and Asian conflicts and non-entanglement in international politics. Although the United States took measures to avoid political and military conflicts across the oceans, it continued to expand economically and protect its interests in Latin America. The leaders of the isolationist movement drew upon history to bolster their position. In his Farewell

Address, President George Washington advocated non-involvement in European wars and politics. The protective expanse of the Atlantic and Pacific Oceans had made it possible for the United States to enjoy a kind of "free security" and remain largely detached from Old World conflicts. During World War I, however, President Woodrow Wilson made a case for U.S. intervention in the conflict and a U.S. interest in maintaining peaceful world order. Nevertheless, the American experience in that war bolsters the arguments of isolationists; they argued that marginal U.S. interests in that conflict did not justify the number of U.S. casualties.

The League of Nations was the first worldwide intergovernmental organization whose principal mission was maintaining world peace. It was founded on 10 January 1920 by the Paris Peace Conference that ended the First World War. The main organization ceased operations on 20 April 1946, but many of its components were relocated to the new United Nations.

The League's primary goals were stated in its Covenant. They included preventing wars through collective security and disarmament and settling international disputes through negotiation and arbitration. Its other concerns included labor conditions, just treatment of native inhabitants, human and drug trafficking, the arms trade, global health, prisoners of war, and protection of minorities in Europe. The Covenant of the League of Nations was signed on 28 June 1919 as Part I of the Treaty of Versailles, and it became effective together with the rest of the Treaty on 10 January 1920. In 1919 U.S. president Woodrow Wilson won the Nobel Peace Prize for his role as the leading architect of the League, even though Americans never joined the league.

At its greatest extent, from 28 September 1934 to 23 February 1935, it had 58 members. After some notable successes and some early failures in the 1920s, the League ultimately proved incapable of preventing aggression by the Axis powers in the 1930s. The organization's credibility was weakened by the fact that the United States never joined the League, and the Soviet Union joined late and was soon expelled. Germany withdrew from the League, as did Japan, Italy, Spain, and others. The onset of the Second World War in 1939 showed that the League had failed its primary purpose; it was inactive until its abolition. The League lasted for 26 years; the United Nations (UN) replaced it in 1946 and inherited several agencies and organizations founded by the League.

## Inter-War Period

It is not our purview here to compare American militarism to the other early 20th-century imperialist powers such as Japan, Great Britain, France, or Italy. However, below is a more detailed listing of American militarism projected globally between the years following World War I and World War II. It is for historians and readers to judge whether militarism was required for peaceful ends or other more pernicious goals such as imperialistic empire-building.

**1917–1922**: Cuba: U.S. forces protected American interests during the insurrection and subsequent unsettled conditions. Most of the

United States armed forces left Cuba by August 1919, but two companies remained at Camaguey until February 1922.[50]

**1918–1919**: Mexico: After the withdrawal of the Pershing expedition, U.S. troops entered Mexico in pursuit of bandits at least three times in 1918 and six times in 1919. In August 1918, American and Mexican troops fought at Nogales, Battle of Ambos Nogales. The incident began when German spies plotted an attack with the Mexican Army on Nogales, Arizona. The fighting began when a Mexican officer shot and killed a U.S. soldier on American soil. A full-scale battle then ensued, ending with a Mexican surrender.

**1918–1920**: Panama: U.S. forces were used for police duty according to treaty stipulations, at Chiriqui, during election disturbances and subsequent unrest.

**1919**: Dalmatia (Croatia): U.S. forces landed at Trau at the request of Italian authorities to police order between the Italians and Serbs.

**1919**: Turkey: Marines from USS *Arizona* were landed to guard the U.S. Consulate during the Greek occupation of Constantinople.

**1919**: Honduras: From September 8 to 12, a landing force was sent ashore to maintain order in a neutral zone during an attempted revolution.

**1920**: Guatemala: From April 9 to 27, U.S. forces protected the American Legation and other American interests, such as the cable

---

[50] https://en.wikipedia.org/wiki/Timeline_of_United_States_military_operations

station, during a period of fighting between Unionists and the Government of Guatemala.

**1920–1922**: Russia (Siberia): From February 16, 1920, to November 19, 1922, a Marine guard was sent to protect the United States radio station and property on the Russian Island, Bay of Vladivostok.

**1921**: Panama and Costa Rica: American naval squadrons demonstrated in April on both sides of the Isthmus to prevent war between the two countries over a boundary dispute.

**1922**: Turkey: In September and October, a landing force was sent ashore with Greek and Turkish authorities' consent to protect American lives and property when the Turkish nationalists entered İzmir (Smyrna).

**1924**: Honduras: From February 28 to March 31 and September 10 to 15, U.S. forces protected American lives and interests during election hostilities.

**1925**: Honduras: From April 19 to 21, U.S. forces protected foreigners at La Ceiba during a political upheaval.

**1925**: Panama: From October 12 to 23, strikes and rent riots led to about 600 American troops landing to keep order and protect American interests.

**1926–1933**: Nicaragua: From May 7 to June 5, 1926, August 27, 1926, to January 3, 1933, the coup d'état of General Emiliano Chamorro Vargas aroused revolutionary activities leading to the landing of American marines to protect the interests of the United

States. United States forces came and went intermittently until January 3, 1933.

**1932**: United States: "Bonus Army" of 17,000 WWI veterans plus 20,000 families cleared from Washington and then Anacostia flats "Hooverville" by 3rd Cavalry and 12th Infantry Regiments under Gen. Douglas MacArthur and Major Dwight D Eisenhower, July 28.

**1933**: Cuba: During a revolution against President Gerardo Machado naval forces demonstrated but no landing was made.

**1940**: Newfoundland,Bermuda, St.Lucia,– Bahamas, Jamaica, Anti gua, Trinidad,and British Guiana: Troops were sent to guard air and naval bases obtained under lease by negotiation with the United Kingdom. These were sometimes called lend-lease bases but were under the destroyers-for-bases deal.

**1941**: Greenland: Greenland was taken under the protection of the United States in April.

**1941**: Netherlands (Dutch Guiana): In November, the President ordered American troops to occupy Dutch Guiana, but by agreement with the Netherlands government in exile, Brazil cooperated to protect the aluminum ore supply from the bauxite mines in Suriname.

**1941**: Iceland: Iceland was taken under the protection of the United States without the consent of its government replacing British troops for strategic reasons.

## The Beginning of World War II in Asia

On December 7, 1941, following the Japanese bombing of Pearl Harbor, the United States declared war on Japan. Three days later, after Germany and Italy declared war on it, the United States became fully engaged in the Second World War. In an ominous prelude to World War II, Japanese forces swept into Eastern China in 1937 and laid waste to Shanghai and Nanking. The Second Sino-Japanese War (1937–1945) was a military conflict that was primarily waged between the Republic of China and the Empire of Japan. Japan's leaders proclaimed this to be the first step in creating a "new order" that would rid Asia and the Pacific of Western colonial and imperial influence; Japan annexed Korea in 1910 and took control of Manchuria in 1931.

In 1894, Japan began its military aggression and colonial war. Japan forced China to cede Taiwan and the Liaodong Peninsula, and dominated Korea, making it a Japanese colony. 20,000 Dalian people were brutally massacred by the Japanese army in Port Arthur (now Dalian). After Japan succeeded in a series of barbaric wars of aggression against China and Korea, its ambitions grew. In 1905, Japan defeated the Russian Empire during the Russo-Japanese war. The attack on the Russian Navy moored at Port Arthur before the formal announcement of war was so successful. The arrogance of militarism was growing. Japan was trying to annex Asia, dominate the world, and gradually become the birthplace of World War II. In 1941, Japan used the same tactic to attack America's naval base in Pearl Harbor, Hawaii.

After 1931 Japan revaluated its strategic plan and focused its power on expanding its empire in the Northeast. Late in 1931, Japan experimented with its power, invading the Chinese province of Manchuria and setting up a violently repressive puppet state. In its invasion of Manchuria, Japan had set into motion the first acts of the steps toward World War II that would start about a decade later.

The beginning of the Second Sino-Japanese War is conventionally dated to the Marco Polo Bridge Incident on 7 July 1937. At that time, the Japanese army invaded Wanping City in Beijing under the pretext of the disappearance of soldiers during the exercise. This was a blatant act of aggression and was rejected by the Chinese defenders. The Japanese army immediately launched a large-scale military offensive and occupied Beijing, Tianjin, and other large areas of northern China in less than three months. This full-scale war between the Chinese and the Empire of Japan is often regarded as the beginning of World War II in Asia. China fought Japan with aid from the Soviet Union, the United Kingdom, and the United States. Because China's national strength, technology, and military equipment lag behind Japan, China's situation in this war were very difficult. Large swathes of the country were destroyed, and countless people were slaughtered. The allied countries were also practically helpless. America was not prepared to offer military backing to intervene, it however issued 'The Stimson Doctrine,' which reinforced the allied interest in China.

In August 1937, the Japanese army invaded Shanghai, where they met strong resistance and suffered heavy casualties. The battle was bloody as both sides faced attrition in urban hand-to-hand combat.

By mid-November, the Japanese had captured Shanghai with the help of naval and aerial bombardment. The General Staff Headquarters in Tokyo initially decided not to expand the war due to the high casualties incurred and the low morale of the troops. However, Japan tried in vain to destroy the will of the Chinese military and civilians to resist by occupying Nanjing, the capital of China at that time. On December 1, headquarters ordered the Central China Area Army and the 10th Army to capture Nanjing. The catastrophe of the Nanjing people began.

The Nanjing Massacre or the Rape of Nanjing was the mass murder and rapes of Chinese civilians in Nanjing, the capital of the Republic of China, immediately after the Battle of Nanking in the Second Sino-Japanese War, by the Imperial Japanese Army. Beginning on December 13, 1937, the massacre lasted six weeks. The Japanese perpetrators also committed other war crimes, such as mass rape, looting, and arson. The massacre was one of the worst atrocities committed during World War II.

Due to a myriad of factors, death toll estimates vary from 40,000 to over 300,000, with rape cases ranging from 20,000 to over 80,000 cases. However, most credible scholars support the validity of the International Military Tribunal for the Far East and its findings, which estimate at least 200,000 murders and at least 20,000 cases of rape. Japanese "successes" in Asia emboldened it to make an

'Axis' treaty with the German dictator Adolph Hitler and to attack America on December 7, 1941.[51]

## America and Europe Before 1941

During World War II, the United States began to provide significant military supplies and other assistance to the Allies in September 1940, even though the United States did not enter the war until December 1941. Much of this aid flowed to the United Kingdom and other nations already at war with Germany and Japan through an innovative program known as Lend-Lease.

When war broke out in Europe in September 1939, U.S. President Franklin D Roosevelt declared that while the United States would remain neutral in law, he could "not ask that every American remain neutral in thought as well." Roosevelt himself made significant efforts to help nations engaged in the struggle against Nazi Germany and wanted to extend a helping hand to those countries that lacked the supplies necessary to fight against the Germans. The United Kingdom, in particular, desperately needed help, as it was short of hard currency to pay for the military goods, food, and raw materials it needed from the United States.

It often seems that modern-day American leaders and many of the American people are eager to intervene in conflicts that, ultimately, may have nothing to do with the country. Over 75 years ago, the

---

[51] "Axis Aggression," National Museum of American History, November 9, 2021, https://americanhistory.si.edu/price-of-freedom/world-war-ii/axis-aggression.

exact opposite could be said. With Europe locked in battle, President Franklin D. Roosevelt supported the idea of America going to war, giving Great Britain the backing it needed, but FDR faced his own struggles. The United States didn't want to intervene.

During an emergency cabinet meeting called by Roosevelt immediately after the war erupted in Europe, it was agreed that the United States would remain an outside influence unless directly threatened or attacked.

Even had the government backed the war, the United States was still getting over the turmoil of World War I and the Great Depression. The general public was not ready to join another war, opting for neutrality. A poll taken in 1939, after the outbreak of war, showed that 94% were against going to war.

Even if the United States had wanted to enter the war, its military force was simply not ready. Facing off against millions of Germans, the American military was only about 100,000 strong without a draft. To enter the European crisis would likely mean a complete decimation of America's forces. Beyond a lack of force, the United States military was generally behind on weaponry, with much of it dating back to the First World War. The current force wasn't ready for war against the better-trained Germans. Even if the numbers were there, the preparedness was not.

The war in Europe didn't seem to pose any threat to the American economy, and joining it only served to threaten America's stability. It should be noted that prior to the U.S.'s entry into World War II, there were large rallies of American Nazis, particularly in New York City.

Also, there were numerous successful American companies doing business with Nazi Germany, even IBM. Also, many American political and business leaders were against the U.S.'s entry into the war. Though not actively participating, the U.S. was actually benefiting from the conflict, manufacturing military equipment and vehicles for the Allied forces. Without pumping that money right back into the military, it served to bolster the country's economy.

With one massive attack on American territory in 1941, the entire outlook of the country changed. Patriotism took over, and without pause that 94% opposed to intervention vanished. Congress reversed its vote of neutrality and opted to fight back against would-be aggressors.

On December 8th, 1941, while the wreckage of Pearl Harbor was still smoldering, the decision to go to war with Japan was made, and all of the hesitation and desire for neutrality was no more than a memory.

So, in analyzing America's entry into World War I, can we state that America was not preparing militarily or psychologically to enter the war? But when the U.S. finally entered the war, was it for the purpose of peace? Or was it for revenge?

**America's Role in WW II**

The actual war in Europe began with a series of events:

- Germany took Austria (1938) and the Sudetenland (1938)

- The Munich Pact was created (1938) with England and France agreeing to allow Hitler to keep the Sudetenland as long as no further expansion occurred
- Hitler and Mussolini created the Rome-Berlin Axis military alliance to last 10 years (1939)
- Japan entered an alliance with Germany and Italy (1939)
- The Moscow-Berlin Pact occurred, promising nonaggression between the two powers (1939)
- Hitler invaded Poland (1939)
- England and France declared war on Germany (September 30, 1939)

At this time, and despite President Franklin Roosevelt's desire to help the allied powers of France and Great Britain, the only concession America made was to allow the sale of arms on a "cash and carry" basis.

Hitler continued to expand in Europe, taking Denmark, Norway, the Netherlands, and Belgium. In June 1940, France fell to Germany. The speed of the expansion was noticed in the U.S., and the government began to reinforce the military.

The final break in U.S. isolationism began with the 1941 Lend-Lease Act, whereby America was allowed to "sell, transfer title to, exchange, lease, lend, or otherwise dispose of, to any such government...any defense article." Great Britain promised not to export any of the lend-lease materials. After this, America built a base on Greenland and then issued the Atlantic Charter on August 14, 1941. The document was a joint declaration between Great Britain and the U.S. about the purposes of war against fascism. The Battle of the Atlantic began with German U-boats wreaking havoc and even spread to the East coast of America with the German U-boats sinking some American merchant ships.

American war production — its ability to churn out astounding numbers of bombers, tanks, and warships — was possibly the key war-winning factor, say some historians, who point out that American factories produced more airplanes than all of the other major war powers combined. Without U.S. supplies, the European and Soviet war effort would have been massively diminished. America supplied billions of dollars' worth of guns and artillery, munitions, warplanes, ships, tanks, food, and clothing. American war power greatly contributed to liberating Europe and Asia from the Nazi Germans and the imperialist Japanese.

**Hiroshima**

The American atomic bombings of Hiroshima and Nagasaki occurred Aug 6, 1945 – Aug 9, 1945. President Truman stated that his decision to drop the bomb was purely military. A Normandy-type amphibious landing would have cost an estimated million American casualties. Truman believed that the bombs saved Japanese lives as well. Prolonging World War II after VE Day (Victory in Europe Day on May 8, 1945) war was not an option for the President. It was argued that a bloody invasion and round-the-clock conventional bombing would have led to a far higher death toll. So the atomic weapons actually saved thousands of American and millions of

Japanese lives, and the bombs were the best means to bring about unconditional surrender, which is what the US leaders wanted. However, the overwhelming historical evidence from American and Japanese archives indicates that Japan would have surrendered that August, even if atomic bombs had not been used — and documents prove that President Truman and his closest advisors knew it. General Curtis LeMay, chief of the Air Forces, said, "The war would have been over in two weeks without the Russians entering and without the atomic bomb." However, the general interpretation of the covert enemy intercepts at the time was that Japan might be on the road to surrender, and they perceived there was a sympathetic "peace party" in their high command, but that Japan was ultimately not yet ready to accept unconditional surrender. Whatever the debate, it is universally accepted that the atomic bombings of Hiroshima and Nagasaki were the reason for Japan's surrender and the end of World War II. However, historians have questioned whether the bombings were also intended as a powerful nuclear warning to the Soviet Union.

Here again, we may ask, did America enter World II for the reason of peace (along with the horrific bombings of Hiroshima and Nagasaki), or were there mainly militaristic and imperialist motives for America to enter and help win World War II? Was war the means to peace?

## The Marshall Plan[52]

It could be questioned here also if the Marshall Plan implemented by the United States had peaceful or militaristic motives. Let's examine the facts. The Marshall Plan, also known as the European Recovery Program, was a U.S. program providing aid to Western Europe following the devastation of World War II. It was enacted in 1948 and provided more than $15 billion ($2.321 Trillion in today's value) to help finance rebuilding efforts on the continent. The brainchild of U.S. Secretary of State George C. Marshall, for whom it was named, it was crafted as a four-year plan to reconstruct cities, industries, and infrastructure heavily damaged during the war and to remove trade barriers between European neighbors—as well as foster commerce between those countries and the United States.

In addition to economic redevelopment, one of the stated goals of the Marshall Plan was to halt the spread of communism on the European continent. Implementation of the Marshall Plan has been cited as the beginning of the Cold War between the United States and its European allies and the Soviet Union,

which had effectively taken control of much of central and Eastern Europe and established its satellite republics as communist nations.

Post-war Europe was in dire straits: Millions of its citizens had been killed or seriously wounded in World War II, as well as in related

---

52 History.com Editors, "Marshall Plan," History.com (A&E Television Networks, December 16, 2009), https://www.history.com/topics/world-war-ii/marshall-plan-1.

atrocities such as the Holocaust. Many cities, including some of the leading industrial and cultural centers of Great Britain, France, Germany, Italy, and Belgium, had been destroyed. Reports provided to Marshall suggested that some regions of the continent were on the brink of famine because agricultural and other food production had been disrupted by the fighting.

In addition, the region's transportation infrastructure – railways, roads, bridges, and ports – had suffered extensive damage during airstrikes, and the shipping fleets of many countries had been sunk. In fact, it could easily be argued that the only world power not structurally affected by the conflict was the United States.

The reconstruction coordinated under the Marshall Plan was formulated following a meeting of the participating European states in the latter half of 1947. Notably, invitations were extended to the Soviet Union and its satellite states. However, they refused to join the effort, allegedly fearing U.S. involvement in their respective national affairs.

President Harry Truman signed the Marshall Plan on April 3, 1948, and aid was distributed to 16 European nations, including Britain, France, Belgium, the Netherlands, West Germany, and Norway. To highlight the significance of America's largesse, the billions committed in aid effectively amounted to a generous 5 percent of the U.S. gross domestic product at the time.

The Marshall Plan provided aid to the recipients essentially on a per capita basis, with larger amounts given to major industrial powers, such as West Germany, France, and Great Britain. This was based on the belief of Marshall and his advisors that recovery in these larger nations was essential to overall European stability and economic security.

Here again, we need to question America's motives in setting up and paying for the Marshall Plan: militaristic or peaceful? Factually, America has always been known as the most altruistic and charitable country in the world in comparison to aid given within the U.S. and globally. America has been the world's most generous country over the last 10 years, according to the 2021 Charity Aids Foundation (United Kingdom-based) World Giving Index 10th edition. Was the Marshall Plan simply an American altruistic action, or was it based on an economic equation? Today, the European Union and the United States have the largest bilateral trade and investment relationship in the world and enjoy the most integrated economic relationship in the world. Although overtaken by China in 2021 as the largest EU import source for goods, the US remains the EU's largest trade and investment partner by far. America's motives in setting up and paying for the Marshall Plan: militaristic or peaceful?

## NATO

The Marshall Plan is also considered a key catalyst for forming the North Atlantic Treaty Organization (NATO), a military alliance between North American and European countries established in 1949. The Soviet Union and even after the fall of the Soviet Union, countries politically aligned with the subsequent Russian Federation certainly see NATO as organized for purely militaristic purposes. America is certainly considered NATO's largest military power, with its own vastly stationed military materiel and tens of thousands of troops across Europe to support the defense of Western Europe. Can America's position in NATO be construed objectively as peaceful or militaristic? Some say that the most visible political symbol of the Pax Americana is NATO itself. Note that the Supreme Allied Commander of NATO is always an American, and whose influence always outweighs that of their European partners. Beginning around the Vietnam War, the Pax Americana term started to be used by the critics of American Imperialism. Here in the late 20th-century conflict between the Soviet Union and the United States, the charge of Neocolonialism was often aimed at Western involvement in the affairs of the Third World and other developing nations. NATO became regarded as a symbol of Pax Americana in West Europe.

NATO is an intergovernmental military alliance between 30 member states – 28 European and two North American. NATO is a system of collective security: its independent member states agree to defend each other against attacks by third parties. The combined militaries of all NATO members include around 3.5 million soldiers and personnel. Their combined military spending as of 2020 constituted over 57 percent of the global nominal total. Members have agreed that their aim is to reach or maintain the target defense spending of at least two percent of their GDP by 2024.

NATO formed with twelve founding members and has added new members eight times, most recently when North Macedonia joined the alliance in March 2020. Following the acceptance of their applications for membership in June 2022, Finland and Sweden are anticipated to become the 31st and 32nd members, with their

Accession Protocols to the North Atlantic Treaty now ratified by the existing members. NATO currently recognizes Bosnia, Georgia, and Ukraine as aspiring members. Enlargement has led to tensions with non-member Russia, one of the twenty additional countries participating in NATO's Partnership for Peace program.

During the Cold War, NATO operated as a check on the perceived threat posed by the Soviet Union. The alliance remained in place after the dissolution of the Soviet Union and has been involved in military operations in the Balkans, the Middle East, South Asia, and Africa.

Here too, we can review each case of NATO (led by America) intervention and military deployment to judge if its purpose has been for peaceful or militaristic means.

**United Nations**

After the Second World War, no armed conflict emerged among major Western nations, and no nuclear weapons were used in open conflict. The United Nations was also soon developed after World War II by 51 countries led by the United States, Soviet Union, United Kingdom, and China to help keep peaceful relations between nations countries and committed to maintaining international peace and security, developing friendly relations among nations, and promoting social progress, better living standards, and human rights.[53]

---

[53] "History of the UN Seventieth Anniversary," United Nations, https://www.un.org/un70/en/content/history/index.html.

Due to its unique international character and the powers vested in its founding Charter, the Organization can take action on a wide range of issues and provide a forum for its 193 Member States to express their views through the General Assembly, the Security Council, the Economic and Social Council and other bodies and committees.

The work of the United Nations reaches every corner of the globe. Although best known for peacekeeping, peacebuilding, conflict prevention, and humanitarian assistance, there are many other ways the United Nations and its System (specialized agencies, funds, and programs) affect lives globally to make the world a better place. The Organization works on a broad range of fundamental issues, from sustainable development, environment, and refugees protection, disaster relief, counter-terrorism, disarmament, and non-proliferation, to promoting democracy, human rights, gender equality, and the advancement of women, governance, economic and social development, and international health, clearing landmines, expanding food production, and more, to achieve its goals and coordinate efforts for a safer world for this and future generations.

The UN has 4 main purposes:

- To keep peace throughout the world.
- To develop friendly relations among nations.

- To help nations work together to improve the lives of poor people, to conquer hunger, disease, and illiteracy, and to encourage respect for each other's rights and freedoms.
- To be a center for harmonizing the actions of nations to achieve these goals.

### America's Role in the Founding of the United Nations

The impetus to establish the United Nations stemmed largely from the inability of its predecessor, the League of Nations, to prevent the outbreak of the Second World War. Despite Germany's occupation of several European states, and the League's failure to stop other serious international transgressions in the 1930s, such as Japan's invasion of Manchuria, many international leaders remained committed to the League's ideals. Once World War II began, President Franklin D. Roosevelt determined that U.S. leadership was essential for the creation of another international organization aimed at preserving peace, and his administration engaged in international diplomacy in pursuit of that goal. He also worked to build domestic support for the concept of the United Nations. After Roosevelt's death, President Harry S Truman also assumed the important task of maintaining support for the United Nations and worked through complicated international problems, particularly with the Soviet Union, to make the founding of the new organization possible. After nearly four years of planning, the international community finally established the United Nations in the spring of 1945 in New York City. Undoubtedly, after the devastation of World War II and the military and economic power of the post-war United States, no other nation was able to push forward the founding of the United Nations.

Were the actions of President Roosevelt here altruistic i.e. in the name of peace, or for the purpose of some future militaristic advantage of America?

The governments of the United States, the Soviet Union, the United Kingdom, and China formalized the Atlantic Charter proposals in January 1942, shortly after the United States entered the war. In the Declaration of the United Nations, these major Allied nations, along with 22 other states, agreed to work together against the Axis powers (Germany, Japan, and Italy) and committed in principle to establishing the United Nations after the war.

Learning from Woodrow Wilson's failure to gain Congressional support for the League of Nations, the Roosevelt Administration aimed to include a wide range of administration and elected officials in its effort to establish the proposed United Nations. The State Department played a significant role in this process and created a Special Subcommittee on International Organization in the Advisory Committee on Postwar Plans. In March 1943, Congress drafted a formal proposal to establish a new, more effective international organization. Secretary of State Cordell Hull took the proposal to members of Congress to build bipartisan support for the proposed postwar organization. Consultations between Congress and the Department of State continued into the summer of 1943, and by August, produced a draft United Nations Charter. Congress repeatedly passed resolutions declaring its support for establishing an international organization--and for United States membership in that organization.

The major Allied Powers--the United States, the Soviet Union, the United Kingdom, and China--reiterated their commitment to forming an international organization in the Moscow Declaration of October 30, 1943. Recall that these actions were being undertaken at the height of World War II, with VE Day (Victory Europe) declared on May 8, 1945, and VJ Day (Victory Japan) declared on August 14, 1945.

Representatives from these four countries met at Dumbarton Oaks in Washington, DC, from August 21 through October 7, 1944. The four Allied powers issued a statement of Proposals for the Establishment of a General International Organization, largely based on the draft charter formulated by the State Department's Subcommittee on International Organization in consultation with the U.S. Congress.

The U.S. State Department of State undertook a public relations campaign to build support for the United Nations. The Department worked in concert with interested groups to inform the public about the United Nations and even dispatched officials around the country to answer questions about the proposed organization.

The basic framework for the proposed United Nations rested on President Roosevelt's vision that the United States, the Soviet Union, the United Kingdom, and China would provide leadership in the postwar international system. It was these four states, with the addition of France, that would assume permanent seats in the otherwise rotating membership of the United Nations Security Council. At its first session, on February 14, 1946, the United Nations General Assembly voted to establish its permanent headquarters in New York City. In a world emerging from the overwhelming conflict of World War II, the United Nations seemed to represent the hope that such devastation would not recur. The Universal Declaration of Human Rights, adopted by the General Assembly in 1948, symbolized this optimism and idealism.

The peacekeeping history of the United Nations will be reviewed in a subsequent chapter.

**Korean War**

World War II divided Korea into the northern half and an American-occupied southern half, divided at the 38th parallel. The Korean War (1950-1953) began when the North Korean army crossed the 38th Parallel. As Kim Il-Sung's North Korean army, armed with Soviet tanks, quickly overran South Korea, the United States came to South Korea's aid. General Douglas MacArthur, who had been overseeing the post-WWII occupation of Japan, commanded the US forces, which now began to hold off the North Koreans at Pusan, at the southernmost tip of Korea.

Although Korea was not strategically essential to the United States, the political environment at this stage of the Cold War with the Soviet Union was such that America's policymakers did not want to appear "soft on Communism." Critics of the Korean War have said that nominally, the US intervened as part of a "police action" run by a

United Nations international peace-keeping force, but in actuality, the United Nations was simply being manipulated by U.S. and NATO anti-Communist interests. Were the U.S. and NATO anti-communistic actions taken during the Korean War part of America's post-World War II militaristic and expansionist visions, or was this American-led war expressionism of the United States' earnest quest for global peace?

With the U.S., United Nations, and South Korean (ROK) forces pinned against the sea at Pusan, MacArthur orchestrated a daring amphibious assault on Inchon, a port on the western coast of Korea. Having made this landing, MacArthur crushed the North Korean army in a pincer movement and recaptured Seoul, the capital of South Korea. Instead of being satisfied with his rapid reconquest of South Korea, MacArthur crossed the 38th Parallel and pursued the North Korean army all the way to the northernmost provinces of North Korea.

On September 30, Zhou Enlai, Chinese Premier, delivered a speech and warned the United States: "The Chinese people will never tolerate foreign aggression, nor allow the imperialists to ignore their neighbors' wanton aggression." But MacArthur determined that China would not dare to send troops to confront the United States. Therefore, despite the repeated warnings of the Chinese government, the US military crossed the 38th Parallel on October 1 and occupied Pyongyang on the 19th in an attempt to quickly occupy entire North Korea, and openly claimed: "In history, the Yalu River is not a clear division between China and North Korea. This is an insurmountable obstacle." At the same time, American planes repeatedly invaded China's airspace and bombed the Dandong area, and the war was about to burn to the Yalu River.

On October 8, 1950, the North Korean government requested China to send troops for assistance. At the request of the North Korean government, China decided to "resist America and aid North Korea, protect the homeland and defend the country" and quickly formed the Chinese People's Volunteers to join the war in North Korea. On the evening of October 19, General Peng Dehuai led the Chinese People's Volunteer Army across the Yalu River from Andong, Changdian River Mouth (now Shanghai Mouth), and Ji'an. After the 13th Corps crossed the river, it was reorganized as the headquarters of the Chinese People's Volunteers on October 20. On October 25, the Volunteers started their first battle after garrisoning in Korea. The warring sides fought five consecutive battles from October 25, 1950, to June 10, 1951. The front line was stalemate at the 38th Parallel, with heavy casualties.

Although President Truman hoped to end the war quickly and pressed MacArthur to be more tactful, the brilliant strategist went against presidential orders and continued spouting incendiary lines about his hopes to reunify Korea. After gaining the support of the Joint Chiefs of Staff (JCS), Truman relieved MacArthur of command. The move was extremely unpopular in America; MacArthur was perceived as a popular war hero. Only the support of the JCS saved Truman from impeachment after the firing.

Ridgway took MacArthur's command and held off the Volunteers and North Korea with strong fortifications and entrenchments just north of the 38th Parallel. Both sides of the war were trying to take the initiative, break the deadlock, and seek a more favorable position for themselves. Peace negotiations dragged on at Kaesong, then moved and continued to drag at Panmunjom through 1951 and 1952. The U.S. tried using strategic bombing to intimidate the Volunteers and North Korea into negotiating a peace treaty, but they wouldn't budge, particularly regarding POW (Prisoner of War) repatriation. Neither side wanted to appear weak, so the talks went on, occasionally breaking down for months. Only after General Dwight D. Eisenhower, who was a war hero and was unafraid of Republican criticism (since he himself was a Republican), became President could the U.S. make substantial concessions to the Communists.

In 1953 an armistice was signed at Panmunjom that ended the hostilities of the Korean War, returning Korea to a divided status essentially the same as before the war. However, a peace treaty was never signed. Neither the Korean War nor its outcome did much to lessen the era's Cold War tension or to provide a true and lasting peace on the Korean peninsula. What did this American-led war do toward a peaceful resolution? Would peace have come to the Korean peninsula if the American-led war had not occurred? If yes, then what kind of peace?

## Central Intelligence Agency Military Interventions[54]

The agency was created by the National Security Act of 1947 to expand the government's espionage capacities and ability to thwart communism through covert activities. CIA functions included propaganda, sabotage, economic warfare, and support for anti-Communist forces worldwide. The CIA is supposed to stop threats to the United States before they happen, further U.S. national collection of foreign intelligence; produce objective analysis; and conduct covert action, as directed by the president.

CIA does not make policy or policy recommendations. Instead, the agency serves as an independent source of information for people who do make policy decisions.

The United States has invaded or fought in 84 of the 193 countries recognized by the United Nations and has been militarily involved with 191 of 193 – a staggering 98% of the world's nations. The Central Intelligence Agency has been involved in every one of those military conflicts or interventions. There are only three countries in the world that America hasn't invaded or has never seen a U.S. military presence: Andorra, Bhutan, and Liechtenstein. Below is a short history of only a few of the CIA's most notable interventions. The reader can decide which of these CIA actions led to peaceful or violent results for the participants affected by these actions.

---

[54] https://www.wearethemighty.com/popular/countries-america-hasnt-invaded/

**CUBA: 1959 - 1961** The U.S. government rejected Cuban President Fidel Castro's request for financial help after the overthrow of Cuban dictator Fulgencio Batiste. Castro and his government turned to the Soviet Union for help. President Eisenhower directed the CIA to begin preparations to invade Cuba and overthrow the Castro regime. On April 15, 1961, the CIA used obsolete World War II B-26 bombers and painted them to look like Cuban air force planes to bomb air force Cuban targets. The bombers missed many of their targets and left most of Castro's air force intact. Later that year, the Bay of Pigs Invasion was a failed attack launched by the CIA during the Kennedy administration to overthrow Fidel Castro. That mission and other CIA operations in Cuba continued to fail.

**BOLIVIA: 1971** A CIA "Brain trust" was formed for the specific purpose of gathering together exiled leaders of several Latin American countries. Victor Paz Estenssoro, former President of Bolivia, was contacted by the Agency while residing in Lima, Peru. A revolt was arranged to return Paz to power. But the agency's plans went unexpectedly awry when Colonel Hugo Banzer took over the office just prior to Paz's triumphant return.

**BRITISH GUIANA: 1962-66** CIA operations in British Guiana revealed the extent to which the Agency has penetrated the mainstream of American life. Cheddi Jagan, the Marxist-oriented Premier of British Guiana was not trusted by the US. Through operatives in AFL-CIO affiliated unions, the CIA supported lengthy strikes in this small South American country in their eventually successful effort to overthrow Jagan. Approximately $1,000,000 of the American union and government money was channeled through the CIA-controlled affiliate unions.

**BRAZIL: 1964** The democratically elected leftist President Joao Goulart government took office in 1961, and that began the process of the C.I.A.'s work in backing the military coup forces that overthrew Goulart in 1964. They sent U.S. naval tankers loaded with petroleum, oil, and lubricants from Aruba to Santos, Brazil; assembling 110 tons of ammunition and other equipment for pro-coup forces; and dispatching a naval brigade including an aircraft carrier, several destroyers, and escorts to be positioned off the coast of Brazil. General Castello Branco led the coup and served as the first president of the military dictatorship that ruled Brazil brutally until 1985.

**CHILE: 1973** When Marxist-leaning Salvador Allende was elected President of Chile, the CIA, ordered by President Nixon, engineered the Chilean military coup d'état a military coup that deposed the Popular Unity government of Allende. The U.S. feared that Allende would push Chile into socialism and therefore lose all of the US investments made in Chile. The brutal dictator General Augusto Pinochet ruled Chile with right-wing policies friendly to the U.S. until 1990 (17 years).

**CONGO:** The CIA, fearing Soviet influence on the new republic, chose to support Joseph Mobutu as their champion over Patrice Lumumba, whom the agency claimed was op much influenced by the Communists. Although there is no direct evidence, there have been many implications that the CIA was instrumental in Lumumba's murder.

**COSTA RICA: 1954-56** Jose Figueres was a moderate socialist who became President of this small democratic country in an open election in 1953. His presence was particularly bothersome to the CIA, and the agency to get rid of Figueres engineered a twofold plan; first, to link Figueres with the Communist party of the country. The CIA failed entirely to remove Figueres from office, and Costa Rica remained a democracy.

**DOMINICAN REPUBLIC: 1962** Through contacts with the CIA made by the American Consulate, two prominent landowners and former politicians conspired with the help of the CIA to assassinate Rafael Trujillo, the dictator of this small Caribbean nation. President Dwight D. Eisenhower believed that Trujillo was just as bad as Castro, and if left alone, he would turn the Dominican Republic into another bastion of communism in the Western Hemisphere. Eisenhower ordered the CIA to mount a covert operation to help the anti-Trujillo elements in the country to overthrow the bothersome dictator. After Trujillo's assassination, President Lyndon Johnson dispatched a force of 22,000 American troops to restore order there and work with a new president, more friendly to American Caribbean political aims.

**EGYPT: 1952** Seeing no advantage in supporting the decaying monarchy of King Farouk, the CIA played an important role in support of the revolt that placed General Naguib and Gamal Abdul Nasser at the head of the country. Nasser, though, proved to be more independent than the US government would have liked; so the State Department convinced President Eisenhower to refuse American aid in building the Aswan Dam.

**GUATEMALA: 1954** One of the most tragic examples of CIA intervention in foreign affairs was the Guatemalan Revolution of 1954. Jacobo Arbenz Guzman, the popularly elected socialist President of the small country was a man marked by the CIA. Guzman had become too friendly with the Soviet Union and had committed the unpardonable sin of expropriating 225,000 acres of United Fruit Company holdings. The U.S. started to move against Guzman in June of 1954, with the CIA directing the action. The CIA supported Carlos Castillo-Armas, an American-trained Guatemalan Colonel, and the agency trained armed men in Honduras which eventually caused the downfall of the Arbenz government. Thereafter, Castillo-Armas' repressive regime took over, fully sanctioned by the CIA. The brutal Guatemalan Civil War was a civil war in Guatemala fought from 1960 to 1996 between the government of Guatemala and various leftist rebel groups.

**INDONESIA: 1958** Washington became annoyed at President Sukarno's leftist tendencies. Sukarno was an Indonesian statesman, orator, revolutionary, and nationalist who was the first president of Indonesia, serving from 1945 to 1967. He had become friendly with the Soviets, began expropriating huge tracts of former Dutch properties, and welcomed a Communist coalition into his Jakarta government. With the wild riches of the Indonesian Archipelago at stake, the CIA took to the air to strike at the Sukarno government.

The U.S. State Department denied everything while the CIA flew its B-26 bombers out of the southern Philippines, raining bombs on the small islands populated by Indonesians partial to Sukarno.

**IRAN: 1953** Mohammed Mossadegh, the Shah-appointed Premier of Iran, bowed to popular sentiment and nationalized the British-owned Anglo-Iranian Oil Company in 1953. The action spawned a boycott of Iranian oil, and the economy began to falter. In the face of these conditions, the British and American governments decided that Mossadegh would be better done away with. Kermit Roosevelt, the grandson of Teddy, illegally entered the country and began organizing CIA operatives to overthrow Mossadegh. Roosevelt did his job well. Mossadegh was promptly arrested, and the Shah returned from unofficial exile in Rome. The incident also worked well for American business. The British lost their monopoly, and a consortium of Gulf Oil, Standard Oil, and Mobil Oil received 40 percent of the concession in reorganizing the former company. Roosevelt later left the CIA officially to take a position with Gulf Oil. The overthrow of Mossadegh and the installation of West-friendly Shah Reza Pahlavi and his brutal, repressive regime (1954 – 1979) led to his eventual overthrow and brought in the current Iran government of the religious mullahs.

**IRAQ: 1958** The CIA was less successful in Iraq than it was in Iran in 1953. The revolution killed King Feisal, but the new government faced a series of revolts from various tribal factions who were angered at the murder of Feisal. This instability was encouraged by the CIA, which actively supported the tribes. Because of the oil companies, it was mandatory to maintain a friendly pro-Western government in Iraq, so the CIA worked to offset the Arab Unity cries beaming from Radio Cairo by setting up many of their own clandestine stations.

**JORDAN: 1958** King Hussein's pro-Western sentiments had shackled pro-Arab factions within the country and weakened the all-Arab alliance. The CIA stayed in Jordan to protect Hussein and successfully repulsed two separate rebellions against the crown.

**LAOS: 1960-present** Since the French withdrawal from Indo-China in 1954, Laos has seen the CIA involved in every aspect of espionage activity until the defeat of the U.S. in Vietnam in 1973. In December 1959, the high-living right-wing military leader, Phoumi No souvan, was assisted by the CIA in overthrowing the US State Department-supported government of Phoui Sananikone. Using rigged elections in April 1960, the CIA could keep Nosouvan in power. When Nosouvan himself was overthrown by a determined young paratrooper, the CIA assisted Nosouvan in setting up his military government further down the Mekong in the province of Savannaket. The State Department sided with the paratrooper, Kong Le.

**PORTUGUESE ANGOLA AND MOZAMBIQUE: 1965** A number of planes with military supplies and advisors were flown covertly from the United States to Portugal for use against Black liberation movements in these countries.

**URUGUAY: 1969-71** Using martial law to quell the student and worker disturbances in this bankrupt country, President Jorge Pacheco Areco, with the assistance of in-country CIA operatives, remained in his presidential position.

**VIETNAM: 1955 - 1973** The CIA had been involved in a myriad of activities since the CIA's predecessor-the Office of Secret Services-left the Indochinese theater soon after WW II. The Agency's influence permeated the entire range of US policy in Vietnam. It was the CIA which at first developed the "intimate" relationship between President Diem and Madame Nhu. It was also the CIA that plotted with the Buddhists several years later to have Diem assassinated.

## President Eisenhower's Warning

President Dwight D. Eisenhower's farewell address to the nation was delivered in a television broadcast on January 17, 1961. General Eisenhower had led Allied forces to victory against the Nazis. So this speech is especially important coming from a leader who knew intimately both the U.S. military and the U.S. government. Perhaps best known for advocating that the nation guard against the potential influence of the military–industrial complex, a term he is credited with coining, he famously said:

“In the councils of government, we must guard against the acquisition of unwarranted influence, whether sought or unsought, by the military-industrial complex. The potential for the disastrous rise of misplaced power exists and will persist. We must never let the weight of this combination endanger our liberties or democratic processes. We should take nothing for granted. Only an alert and knowledgeable citizenry can compel the proper meshing of the huge industrial and military machinery of defense with our peaceful methods and goals, so that security and liberty may prosper together."[55]

This famous speech is generally understood to warn the American people of the dangers of allowing a Military-Industrial Complex to take control of the United States. The Military-Industrial Complex is a term that denotes a symbiotic relationship between a nation's military, economy, and politics.

This warning, unfortunately, has not been heeded. From recent reports, during the five-year period from 2013-2017, there were 1,059 criminal cases of defense contracting fraud resulting in the conviction of 1,087 defendants, including 409 businesses, according to a Department of Defense report to Congress. There were another 443 fraud-related civil cases resulting in judgments against 546 defendants. The value of those contracts exceeded $334 billion, according to the Department of Defense report.

During that same period, the Department of Defense entered into more than 15 million contracts with contractors who had been indicted, fined, and/or convicted of fraud, or who reached settlement agreements.

---

[55]https://www.archives.gov/milestone-documents/president-dwight-d-eisenhowers-farewell-address

“Simply put, the Pentagon continues to be riddled with waste, fraud, and abuse of taxpayer funds to a degree unmatched across the federal government,” Senator Bernard Sanders (D. VT), who was the committee head investigating Department of Defense fraud scandals said in 2017. “It is unacceptable that the Department of Defense continues to lose vast sums of taxpayer money because of fraud perpetrated by major defense contractors. Procurement fraud includes, but is not limited to, cost and labor mischarging, defective pricing, price fixing, bid rigging, and defective and counterfeit parts,” quoted from the report by the Department of Defense Inspector General. Senator Sanders added, “This has got to end!” He also said, “The potential damage from procurement fraud extends well beyond finances. This crime poses a serious threat to the Department of Defense’s ability to achieve its objectives and can undermine the safety and operational readiness of the warfighter.”

Karl Marx, the great Communist writer famously reversed a capitalist meme. Capitalists often say that in economics, demand drives supplies. However, Marx stated that the truth is in capitalist systems, supplies drive demand. He meant that capitalists have to keep creating demand in order to keep their factories and income churning. Does this apply to the American (and other) military-industrial symbioses?

It should be noted that President Eisenhower also initiated the program known as ‘Atoms for Peace’ in 1953. The United States proposed to share non-military nuclear technology, training, and materials with nations around the world in an effort to win hearts and minds (and dominate the nuclear market).

**Vietnam War**

The Gulf of Tonkin Incident occurred in August 1964. North Vietnamese warships purportedly attacked United States warships, the U.S.S. *Maddox* and the U.S.S. *C. Turner Joy*, on two separate occasions in the Gulf of Tonkin, a body of water neighboring modern-day Vietnam. The Gulf of Tonkin Resolution, passed by the U.S. Congress soon after the incident, effectively launched America's full-scale involvement in the Vietnam War.

Historians have long suspected that the second attack in the Gulf of Tonkin was a "false flag" attack that actually never occurred and that the resolution was based on faulty evidence. But no declassified information had suggested that Defense Secretary Robert McNamara, nor President Lyndon Johnson, or anyone else in the decision-making process had intentionally misinterpreted the intelligence concerning the 4 August incident. More than 40 years after the events, that all changed with the release of the nearly 200 documents related to the Gulf of Tonkin incident and transcripts from the Johnson Library.

These new documents and tapes reveal what historians could not prove at the time of the initiation of the war: There was not a second attack on U.S. Navy ships in the Tonkin Gulf in early August 1964. Furthermore, the evidence suggests disturbing and deliberate attempts by Secretary of Defense McNamara to distort the evidence and mislead Congress.

What led to the U.S. entry into war with Vietnam? To answer this question more completely, we have to go back to the French colonization of Vietnam that began in 1858. French colonists were interested in acquiring land, exploiting labor, exporting resources, and making a profit, particularly from the large rice and rubber plantations. Local farmers were forced to labor on these plantations in difficult and dangerous conditions.

When Japan formally surrendered to the Allies on September 2, 1945, Vietnam Communist leader Ho Chi Minh proclaimed the independent Democratic Republic of Vietnam. French forces seized southern Vietnam and opened talks with the Vietnamese communists. These talks collapsed in 1946, and French warships bombarded the northern Vietnamese city of Haiphong, killing thousands.

In response, the Viet Minh of North Vietnam launched an attack against the French in Hanoi on December 19, 1946—the beginning of the First Indochina War. During the eight-year war, Mao Zedong's Chinese communists supported the Viet Minh, while the United States aided the French and anti-communist Vietnamese forces. In 1954, the French suffered a major defeat at Dien Bien Phu, in northwest Vietnam, prompting peace negotiations and the division of Vietnam along the 17th parallel at a conference in Geneva. Vietnam was divided into northern and southern regions, with Ho Chi Minh in command of North Vietnam and Emperor Bao Dai in control of South Vietnam. The Geneva Accords pitted the Soviet Union and the People's Republic of China, backers of North Vietnam against the

U.S. and European backers of South Vietnam. In the late 1950s, Ho Chi Minh organized a Communist guerrilla movement in the South, called the Viet Cong. North Vietnam and the Viet Cong successfully opposed a series of ineffectual U.S.-backed South Vietnam regimes and, beginning in 1964, withstood a decade-long military invasion by the United States.

Why did America want to go to war in Vietnam? Following the end of World War II, Ho Chi Minh reached out to President Harry S Truman for support in ending French rule in Vietnam. Ho Chi Minh referenced the U.N. charter's support of self-government by occupied peoples in World War II. Truman rejected Ho Chi Minh's plea. The U.S. entered the Vietnam War in an attempt to prevent the spread of communism, but foreign policy, economic interests, national fears, and geopolitical strategies also played major roles. Can these American motives be construed as peaceful or militaristic? Was the U.S. more interested in expanding its range of influence, and some would call it neocolonialism, or was this 8 year's military campaign part of an American post-war vision of global peace, security, and prosperity?

It is important to note that massive protests in the United States against the Vietnam War took place from the beginning of the Vietnam War in 1964 to the final American withdrawal from Saigon in 1973. Student protestors were killed by police in these protests, and many college-age male students resisted or evaded the military conscription (or draft, as it was called) to fight in a war 8,000 miles away in an Asian country that most of these young men had never even heard of prior the war.

By disclosure, the writer was one of those young men who evaded conscription by fleeing to and living in Europe for 3 years. Upon his return to the United States, the FBI was searching for him due to his illegal evasion of military duty. By good fortune, this writer was finally able to exonerate himself and not go to fight in Vietnam. It is now known that, during the Vietnam era, approximately 570,000 young American men were classified as draft offenders, and many of them were prosecuted by the government.

The Vietnam War bitterly divided the United States. Most Americans believed in the government's "domino theory," postulating that if Vietnam was lost to the Communists, the other countries nearby in Southeast Asia would also fall to the Communists. This was part of the American belief in the evils of Communism, and the anti-Communist hysteria gripping the American Congress, media, and citizens from the mid-1950s to the late 1990s.

We will examine the horrific losses to Americans and Vietnamese in a subsequent chapter. But how can we judge the Vietnam War within the metric of American militarism or peace by what we know today?

**The Afghanistan War**[56]

The United States went to Afghanistan in 2001 to wage a purported war of self-defense. On September 11, 2001, the al-Qaeda terrorist organization destroyed the World Trade Center in New York City, causing the immediate death of almost 3000 people in New York and during the concurrent attack on the Pentagon military headquarters

---

56 "War in Afghanistan (2001–2021)," Wikipedia (Wikimedia Foundation, October 28, 2022), https://en.wikipedia.org/wiki/War_in_Afghanistan_(2001%E2%80%932021).

near Washington DC. The terrorists could plan and execute such a horrific attack because their Taliban hosts in Afghanistan had given them a safe haven in that country.

In 1997, President George W. Bush and his neo-Conservatives were seen as ideologically aligned with the Project for the New American Century (PNAC). It described the United States as the "world's pre-eminent power" and said that the nation faced a challenge to "shape a new century favorable to American principles and interests." To achieve this goal, the statement's signers called for significant increases in defense spending and for the promotion of "political and economic freedom abroad." It said the United States should strengthen ties with its democratic allies, "challenge regimes hostile to our interests and values," and preserve and extend "an international order friendly to our security, our prosperity, and our principles." Calling for a "Reaganite" policy of "military strength and moral clarity," it concluded that PNAC's principles were necessary "if the United States is to build on the successes of this past century and to ensure our security and our greatness in the next."

In September 2000, PNAC released "Rebuilding America's Defenses," a report that promotes "the belief that America should seek to preserve and extend its position of global leadership by maintaining the preeminence of U.S. military forces." The report also states, "advanced forms of biological warfare that can 'target' specific genotypes may transform biological warfare from the realm of terror to a politically useful tool."

Note that numerous "false flag" theories and scientific studies have been researched and published since the World Trade Center attack that proposes the attack was actually planned and carried out by some "extra-judicial" government agency. The speculative reasoning is that the government was looking for a way to mobilize the American public for the 'war against terrorism' and that an attack by terrorists would be the way to galvanize the country against terrorist movements around the world. That would give the government the needed logic to funding a massive build-up of American military forces, as we have reviewed from previous historical "false flag" theories. And always recall President Eisenhower's portentous warnings against the military-industrial complex that could force the New American Century ideals on planet earth.

The War in Afghanistan lasted from 2001 to 2021. It began when an international military coalition led by the United States launched an invasion of Afghanistan, subsequently toppling the Taliban-ruled Islamic Emirate and establishing the internationally recognized Islamic Republic three years later. The 20-year-long conflict ultimately ended with the 2021 Taliban offensive, which overthrew the Islamic Republic and subsequently re-established the Islamic Emirate. It was the longest war in the military history of the United States.

Following the September 11 attacks, American president George W. Bush demanded that the Taliban, an Afghan Islamist group that had established a *de facto* state over most of Afghanistan, immediately extradite Osama bin Laden to the United States. Bin Laden was wanted for masterminding the attacks, among other previous charges of terrorism, and had been granted asylum by the Taliban in Afghanistan, where he continued to operate freely; the Taliban's refusal to comply with American extradition demands for bin Laden led to the United States' declaration of Operation Enduring Freedom as part of the earlier-declared Global War on Terrorism. Shortly after the invasion of Afghanistan, the Taliban and their allies—namely bin Laden's al-Qaeda—were mostly defeated and expelled from major population centers across the country by American-led forces in support of the Northern Alliance, an anti-Taliban Afghan military front. However, the United States failed to kill or capture bin Laden in the Battle of Tora Bora, after which he relocated to neighboring Pakistan. Despite bin Laden's exit from the country, the American-led coalition of over 40 countries (including all of NATO) remained in Afghanistan, forming a security mission—sanctioned by the United Nations and officially known as the International Security Assistance Force (ISAF)—with the goal of consolidating a new democratic authority in the country that would prevent the return to power of the Taliban and al-Qaeda. At the Bonn Conference, new Afghan interim authorities elected Hamid Karzai to head the Afghan Interim Administration, and an international rebuilding effort was also launched across the entire country.

By 2003, the Taliban had reorganized under their founder, Mullah Omar, and began a widespread insurgency against the new Afghan government as well as against the American-led coalition. Insurgents from the Taliban and other Islamist groups waged asymmetric warfare with guerrilla tactics in the countryside and launched suicide attacks against urban targets—also prominent were "green-on-blue attacks" carried out by Afghan soldiers against international coalition forces, and reprisal attacks against perceived Afghan collaborators. By 2007, fighting between the two sides had escalated to a point where large parts of Afghanistan had been retaken by the Taliban, resulting in a massive ISAF response that increased troops for counter-insurgency operations with a "clear and hold" strategy for villages and towns; the coalition response reached its peak in 2011, when roughly 140,000 foreign troops were operating under the ISAF command across Afghanistan.

Following a covert American military operation that resulted in the killing of Osama bin Laden in the Pakistani city of Abbottabad in May 2011, NATO leaders commenced planning for an exit strategy from Afghanistan, as the goal for the original *casus belli* had been achieved. On 28 December 2014, NATO formally ended ISAF combat operations in Afghanistan and officially transferred full security responsibility to the Afghan government. Unable to eliminate the Taliban through military means, coalition forces (and separately the government of Afghan president Ashraf Ghani) turned to diplomacy to end the conflict. These efforts culminated in the Doha Agreement between the United States and the Taliban in February 2020, which stipulated the withdrawal of all American troops from Afghanistan by April 2021. In exchange for the American withdrawal, the Taliban pledged to prevent militant groups from utilizing Afghan sovereign territory to stage attacks against the United States and its allies. However, the Afghan government was not a party to the deal and rejected its terms regarding the release of prisoners.

The target date for the American withdrawal was later extended to 31 August 2021; the Taliban, after the original deadline of April 2021 had expired, and coinciding with the troop withdrawal, launched a broad offensive throughout the summer, which resulted in their successful capture of most of Afghanistan, including the capital city of Kabul, which was taken on 15 August 2021. On the same day, the last president of the Islamic Republic, Ashraf Ghani, fled the country; the Taliban declared victory, and the war was formally brought to a close. The re-establishment of Taliban rule across Afghanistan was confirmed by the United States, and on 30 August, the last American military aircraft departed from Afghanistan, ending the protracted American-led military presence in the country.

Let us again ask the question regarding America in Afghanistan: Militaristic or Peaceful? Did America attack Afghanistan to prevent more global terrorism by Al-Qaeda? Or did America go to war there out of revenge? Some commentators say the U.S. went to Afghanistan for "nation-building," that is, to create a democratic Afghani political and cultural environment that included women's rights and universal freedoms. Did the trillions of dollars spent in Afghanistan that was voted for by the legislative representatives of the American people for 20 years accomplish the altruistic goals of creating a peaceful and stable nation? Or, by the eventual military triumph of the Taliban, are all these questions moot?

## Gulf War I

At the end of the Iran-Iraq War of 1980–1988, Iraq emerged with its state intact and a reinforced sense of national pride, but laden with massive debts. Iraq had largely financed the war effort through loans, and owed some $37 billion to Gulf creditors in 1990. Iraqi President Saddam Hussein called on the United Arab Emirates and Kuwait to cancel the Iraqi debt they held, arguing that the loans should be considered payments to Iraq for protecting the Arabian Peninsula from Iranian expansionism, but his appeals went unanswered. The Gulf states' refusal to cancel Iraq's war debts contributed to Saddam Hussein's decision to make threats against Iraq's rich but militarily weak, neighbor Kuwait.

On August 2, 1990, a force of one hundred thousand Iraqi troops invaded Kuwait and overran the country in a matter of hours. The invasion of Kuwait led to a United Nations Security Council embargo and sanctions on Iraq and a U.S.-led coalition air and ground war, which began on January 16, 1991, and ended with an Iraqi defeat and retreat from Kuwait on February 28, 1991.

International condemnation of the Iraqi invasion was widespread and virtually unanimous. Within days, the United States led efforts to organize an international coalition, which, working through the United Nations Security Council, passed Resolution 660 demanding Iraq's immediate and unconditional withdrawal, Resolution 661 imposing economic sanctions, and Resolution 663 declaring the annexation of Kuwait null and void.

The United States and Saudi Arabia agreed to deploy U.S. forces to Saudi Arabia to protect the peninsula. At the same time, the United States and the coalition insisted on Iraq's unconditional withdrawal from Kuwait, but Iraq refused to withdraw and began looting Kuwait and destroying its infrastructure.

By October 30, the Bush administration made a decision to push Iraq out of Kuwait by force if necessary. Bush increased the U.S. force presence and petitioned the United Nations for authorization to use force. The result was UN Resolution 678, which authorized the use of force to compel Iraq to withdraw from Kuwait, but gave Iraq a forty-five-day grace period to withdraw. Led by the United States, an international coalition of nations amassed forces in the region to help liberate Kuwait.

After the deadline for withdrawal passed, the coalition led by the United States attacked Iraq by air. Within twenty-four hours, coalition forces controlled the skies and bombarded such strategic sites as the Iraqi command and control facilities, Saddam Hussein's palaces, the Ba'th Party headquarters, power stations, intelligence and security facilities, hydroelectric stations, oil refineries, military-industrial complexes, and Iraq's missile facilities. Coalition aircraft subsequently targeted Iraqi troops in Kuwait

In retaliation, Saddam Hussein launched missile attacks against Israel and on coalition force bases in Saudi Arabia. But Israel refused to retaliate, and coalition forces took the offensive by launching a land campaign that began on February 24 and lasted four days. Comprising forces from thirty-four countries, including a number of Arab countries, the coalition forces liberated Kuwait City and drove Iraqi forces into a retreat.[57]

On March 2, the United Nations Security Council passed Resolution 686, which set forth conditions for a cease-fire. Iraq was obligated to accept its provisions, which included sanctions and payment of reparations for war damages. Iraq was obligated to return property

---

[57]"Why Is the U.S. Sending Troops to Kuwait? - about the Character," https://aboutthecharacter.com/qa/why-is-the-u-s-sending-troops-to-kuwait.html.

stolen from Kuwait. The United States continued to put pressure on Iraq through the United Nations, which passed Security Council Resolution 687, establishing the United Nations Special Commission (UNSCOM) to inspect Iraq's suspected chemical and biological weapons capabilities. The United States subsequently sought to ensure that the trade embargo imposed on Iraq the previous year through Resolution 661 remained in place and that Iraq was stripped of chemical weapons and missiles and its nuclear research capabilities. In the chaos following the war, spontaneous Shiite rebellions in the South and Kurdish unrest in northern Iraq broke out but were eventually suppressed by Saddam Hussein and his Revolutionary Guards.

It may be asked why the United States fought in the Gulf War I. There were four major war aims at the time: complete Iraqi withdrawal from Kuwait, restore Kuwait's government, protect American lives (in particular, free hostages), and "promote the security and the stability of the Persian Gulf." The United States accomplished the first three objectives but not the last.

By looking at the fourth objective, "to promote the security and stability of the Persian Gulf," we may be able to see the real underlying reasons for the U.S. involvement in this war. Why did a majority of the people living in the central part of North America think it was in their interest to send half a million soldiers 6,000 miles away to the Persian Gulf? The simplest answer is one word: oil. To quote one of the better placards at a peace march, "If Kuwait exported broccoli, we wouldn't be there now."

Is oil the whole answer as to why America led the coalition to liberate Kuwait from Saddam Hussein? Other possible aspects of the answer include "a new world order," collective security, interdependence, prevention of regional hegemony, and reversal of perceived American decline.

Most Americans (and other nationalities) want a sense of security -- the absence of threats at home or abroad. Economic well-being is also high on the list. Many jobs that Americans hold and the products they consume depend on the world beyond their borders. But Americans also care about their identity, self-image, and moral values, and they differ in the extent to which they want their government's foreign policy to express their preferences for democracy, human rights, or a sense of national pride. Let us remember that at the time of the Iraqi invasion of Kuwait, as well as today, the Persian Gulf states produce 37% of the world's oil, with Kuwait accounting for 5% of world output. The Persian Gulf states also produce 18% of the world's natural gas. Asia, the epicenter of growth for oil and gas demand globally, is the region most vulnerable to any disruption in supply from the Gulf in the event of war. An estimated 76% of the 17.3 million barrels per day (BPD) of crude and condensate that flowed through the Strait of Hormuz in 2018 went to Asia, accounting for 60% of Persian Gulf oil imports. China, the world's largest crude oil importer, buys about 40% of its crude from the Middle East. Japan buys about 90% of its crude from the Middle East; India buys 60%; South Korea buys 70%; Singapore buys 70%. The European Union Gulf oil imports amount to 18% and 12.4% of the EU's crude oil and natural gas imports respectively. About 9% of U.S. crude oil imports are from Persian Gulf countries.

Therefore, our final question or judgment here should be: Did America lead the coalition of countries in Gulf War I for its own oil importation needs, or to maintain the economic stability of its allies, thereby ensuring its own economic stability in its trade with its trade partners abroad?

**Gulf War II**

In 2002 the new U.S. president, George W. Bush, argued that the vulnerability of the United States following the September 11 attacks of 2001, combined with Iraq's alleged continued possession and manufacture of weapons of mass destruction (an accusation that was later proved erroneous) and its support for terrorist groups—which, according to the Bush administration, included al-Qaeda, the perpetrators of the September 11 attacks—made disarming Iraq a renewed priority.

UN Security Council Resolution 1441, passed on November 8, 2002, demanded that Iraq readmit inspectors and that it comply with all previous resolutions. Iraq appeared to comply with the resolution, but in early 2003 President Bush and British Prime Minister Tony Blair declared that Iraq was actually continuing to hinder UN inspections and that it still retained proscribed weapons. Other world leaders, such as French Pres. Jacques Chirac and German Chancellor Gerhard Schroder, citing what they believed to be increased Iraqi cooperation, sought to extend inspections and give Iraq more time to comply with them.

However, on March 17, seeking no further UN resolutions and deeming further diplomatic efforts by the Security Council futile, Bush declared an end to diplomacy and issued an ultimatum to

Saddam, giving the Iraqi president 48 hours to leave Iraq. The leaders of France, Germany, Russia, and other countries objected to this buildup toward war. When Saddam refused to leave Iraq, the U.S. and allied forces launched an attack on the morning of March 20, 2003. The fight against Saddam Hussein's army ended the following month, in April 2003. However, the U.S. military formally declared the end of the Iraq War in a ceremony in Baghdad on December 15, 2011, as U.S. troops prepared to withdraw from the country.

Following the collapse of the Baathist regime after Saddam's demise, Iraq's major cities erupted in a wave of looting that was directed mostly at government offices and other public institutions, and there were severe outbreaks of violence—both common criminal violence and acts of reprisal against the former ruling clique. Restoring law and order was one of the most arduous tasks for the occupying forces, one that was exacerbated by continued attacks against occupying troops that soon developed into full-scale guerrilla warfare; increasingly, the conflict came to be identified as a civil war, although the Bush administration generally avoided using that term and instead preferred the label "sectarian violence." Coalition casualties had been light in the initial 2003 combat. However, the deaths of U.S. troops soared thereafter. The continuing guerrilla assaults on occupying forces and the incompetence of leaders of the new Iraqi government in the years after the war only compounded the difficulty of rebuilding Iraq and bringing peace to the war-ravaged country.[58]

Unlike the common consent reached in Gulf War I, no broad coalition was assembled to remove Saddam and his Baath Party from power. Although some European leaders voiced their conditional support for the war and none regretted the end of the violent Baathist regime. However, public opinion in Europe and the Middle East was overwhelmingly against the war. Many in the Middle East saw it as a new brand of anti-Arab and anti-Islamic imperialism. Most Arab leaders decried the occupation of a fellow Arab country by foreign troops.

Reaction to the war was mixed in the United States. Though several antiwar protests occurred in American cities in the lead-up to the invasion, many opinion polls showed considerable support for military action against Iraq before and during the war. Surprisingly, American opinions on the war sometimes crossed traditional party lines and doctrinal affiliation, with many to the right of the avowedly conservative Bush seeing the war as an act of reckless internationalism and some to the political left—appalled by the Baathist regime's brutal human rights violations and its consistent aggression—giving grudging support to military action.

The striking fact is that Iraq posed little threat to the US, which was knowable before the war; hence we are left looking for other

---

[58] "Occupation and Continued Warfare," Encyclopædia Britannica, https://www.britannica.com/event/Iraq-War/Occupation-and-continued-warfare.

explanations for the war. The Bush administration's confrontation with Iraq was as much a contest of credibility as it was of military force. Washington claimed that Baghdad harbored ambitions of aggression and continued to develop and stockpile weapons of mass destruction and maintain ties to Al Qaeda, the terrorist group alleged responsible for the 9/11 bombings in New York City.

The evidence is deception and perfidy by the United States leading up to Gulf War II is irrefutable. Armed Forces Chief of Staff, General Colin Powell consciously deceived the world in his 2003 presentation before the U.S. Congress in making a case for war with Saddam Hussein. He fabricated "evidence" and ignored repeated warnings that what he was saying was false.

Powell said about the infamous aluminum tubes purchased by Iraq, supposedly meant for their covert nuclear weapons program:

"We know, we know from sources that a missile brigade outside Baghdad was dispersing rocket launchers and warheads containing biological warfare agent to various locations, distributing them to various locations in western Iraq."

These rocket launchers with biological weapons were never found by U.S. forces during the almost 15 years of war and occupation in Iraq. The claims of an al-Qaeda link with Iraq were challenged by U.S. intelligence officials, and those links were never uncovered.

The Niger uranium forgeries were forged documents initially released in 2001 by SISMI (the former military intelligence agency of

Italy), which seemed to depict an attempt made by Saddam Hussein in Iraq to purchase yellow cake uranium powder from Niger during the Iraq disarmament crisis. Based on these documents and other indicators, the governments of the United States and the United Kingdom asserted that Iraq violated United Nations sanctions against Iraq by attempting to procure nuclear material for the purpose of creating weapons of mass destruction, one of the main reasons for the invasion of Iraq in March 2003.

Historians and analysts are deeply divided over explanations for the war. Compared with other wars, there appears to be an especially radical cleavage between the justifications for war advanced by its proponents, as discussed above and which proved to be hollow, and the actual motives and causes. Since the war, the deceptions practiced by the Bush administration have been exposed. But even before the war, it was clear to ex-weapons inspectors and Iraq specialists that Saddam had no serious WMD capability and certainly not one capable of threatening the US.

Was American global hegemony the reason for Gulf War II? Was securing Iraqi oil for U.S. and western allies the reason for this ultimately irrational and very costly American-led war? Or was the war seen by U.S. government leaders from the point of view of US national interests as embodied in the ideology of the New American Century, particularly after the collapse of the Soviet Union? What is the reader's judgment here? America, militaristic or peaceful?

## Conclusion

In the second half of the 20th century, the USSR and US superpowers were engaged in the Cold War, which can be seen as a struggle between hegemonies for global dominance. After 1945, the United States enjoyed an advantageous position with respect to the rest of the industrialized world. In the Post–World War II economic expansion, the US was responsible for half of the global industrial output, held 80 percent of the world's gold reserves, and was the world's sole nuclear power. The catastrophic destruction of life, infrastructure, and capital during the Second World War had exhausted the imperialism of the Old World, victor and vanquished alike. The largest economy in the world at the time, the United States recognized that it had come out of the war with its domestic infrastructure virtually unscathed and its military forces at unprecedented strength. Military officials recognized the fact that Pax Americana had been reliant on the effective United States air power, just as the instrument of Pax Britannica a century earlier was its sea power. In addition, a *unipolar moment* was seen to have occurred following the collapse of the Soviet Union.

The term *Pax Americana* was explicitly used by John F. Kennedy in the 1960s, who advocated against the idea, arguing that the Soviet bloc was composed of human beings with the same individual goals as Americans and that such a peace based on "American weapons of war" was undesirable:

What kind of peace does America claim to seek in the world? A *Pax Americana* enforced on the world by American weapons of war? Is it peace of the grave or the security of the slave? Genuine peace should be our goal! It is the kind of peace that makes life on earth worth living and the kind that enables men and nations to grow, hope, and build a better life for their children, not merely peace for Americans but peace for all men and women, not merely peace in our time but peace in all time

Currently, the *Pax Americana* is based on the military preponderance beyond challenge by any combination of powers and projection of power throughout the world's *commons*—neutral sea, air, and space. This projection is coordinated by the Unified Command Plan which divides the world into regional branches controlled by a single command. Integrated with it is a global network of military alliances (the Rio Pact, NATO, and bilateral alliances with Japan and several other states) coordinated by Washington in a hub-and-spokes system and worldwide network of several hundreds of military bases and installations.

In contrast to the earlier empires, the scope and pervasiveness of American global power today are unique. Not only does the United States control all the world's oceans, but its military legions are also firmly perched on the western and eastern extremities of Eurasia. American vassals and tributaries, some yearning to be embraced by even more formal ties to Washington, dot the entire Eurasian continent. American global supremacy is buttered by an elaborate system of alliances and coalitions that literally span the globe.

Besides the military foundation, there are significant non-military international institutions backed by American financing and diplomacy (like the United Nations and WTO). The United States invested heavily in programs such as the Marshall Plan and in the reconstruction of Japan, economically cementing defense ties that owed increasingly to the establishment of the Iron Curtain/Eastern Bloc and the widening of the Cold War.

Being in the best position to take advantage of free trade, culturally indisposed to traditional empires, and alarmed by the detonation of the first Soviet atom bomb, the historically non-interventionist US also took a keen interest in developing multilateral institutions which would maintain a favorable world order among them. The International Monetary Fund and International Bank for Reconstruction and Development (World Bank), part of the Bretton Woods system of international financial management was developed and, until the early 1970s, the existence of a fixed exchange rate to the US dollar. The General Agreement on Tariffs and Trade (GATT) was developed and consists of a protocol for the normalization and reduction of trade tariffs.

With the fall of the Iron Curtain and the end of the Cold War, the US maintained significant contingents of armed forces in Europe and East Asia. The institutions behind the Pax Americana and the rise of the United States' unipolar power have persisted into the early 21st century. The ability of the United States to act as "the world's policeman" has been constrained by its own citizens' historical aversion to foreign wars. Though there have been calls for the continuation of military leadership, as stated in "Rebuilding America's Defenses":

Has American peace proven itself peaceful, stable, and durable? Has it, over the past decade, provided the geopolitical framework for widespread economic growth and the spread of American principles of liberty and democracy? Pax Americana will not preserve itself. Americans believe that what is required is a military that is strong and ready to meet both present and future challenges, a foreign policy that boldly and purposefully promotes American principles abroad, and national leadership that accepts the United States' global responsibilities.

This is reflected in U.S. research of American 'exceptionalism' which shows that there is an indication that the U.S. must lead an 'American peace,' but resentments have arisen within the U.S. and globally at a country's or global dependence on American military protection, due to disagreements with United States foreign policy or the presence of American military forces.[59]

Hubert Védrine, the French Socialist politician and former Foreign Minister, describes the U.S. as a hegemonic hyperpower, while the U.S. political scientists John Mearsheimer and Joseph Nye counter that the US is not a true hegemony because it does not have the resources to impose a proper, formal, global rule despite its political and military strength. The US is economically equal to China and Europe and thus cannot rule the international stage. Several other countries are either emerging, also with global aspirations of power and influence.

Historian Joseph Hudson posits the United States as a true hegemony or empire but that the United States must not cultivate a

---

59 "Project for the New American Century," Citizendium, https://en.citizendium.org/wiki/Project_for_the_New_American_Century.

mental view toward world settlement that will enable it to impose its own terms, amounting to the era of US global supremacy. America must not grow into a tree that will overshadow the globe with its foliage. The tendency toward global unification towers up, ready to gather the separate national states together under one banner and blanket, that of the United States.

Pax Americana can be established and maintained only by force, only by means of a new, gigantic imperialism operating with the instrumentalities of militarism and the other concomitants of imperialism. The way to dominion is through the empire, and the price of dominion is the empire, and the empire generates its own opposition, within the empire and from without.

Of course, enemies of the United States have shaken their fists at its "imperialism" for decades. What is more surprising, and much newer, is that the notion of an American empire has suddenly become a live debate inside the United States due to political sectors that eschew the human, material, and financial costs of maintaining an empire.

Peter Bender, in his 2003 article "America: The New Roman Empire," summarized: "When politicians or professors are in need of a historical comparison in order to illustrate the United States' incredible might, they almost always think of the Roman Empire." The article abounds with analogies:

1. "When they later extended their power to overseas territories, they shied away from assuming direct control wherever possible." In the Hellenistic world, Rome withdrew its legions after three

wars and instead settled for the role of all-powerful patron and arbitrator.

The factor for the overseas engagement is the same in both cases: the seas or oceans ceased to offer protection, or so it seemed.

Rome and America both expanded to achieve security. Like concentric circles, each circle needing security demanded the occupation of the next larger circle. The Romans made their way around the Mediterranean, driven from one challenger to their security to the next. The struggles brought the Americans to Europe and East Asia; the Americans soon wound up all over the globe, driven from one attempt at containment to the next. The boundaries between security and power politics gradually blurred. The Romans and Americans both eventually found themselves in a geographical and political position that they had not originally desired but which they then gladly accepted and firmly maintained.

2. "Both claimed the unlimited right to render their enemies permanently harmless." Postwar treatments of Carthage, Macedon, Germany, and Japan are similar.

3. "They became protective lords after each act of assistance provided to other states; in effect, they offered protection and gained control. The protected were mistaken when they assumed that they could use Rome or America to their own ends without suffering a partial loss of their sovereignty."

4. "World powers without rivals are a class unto themselves. They no longer know any foes, just rebels, terrorists, and rogue states. They no longer fight, merely punish. They no longer wage wars but merely create peace. They are honestly outraged when vassals fail to act as vassals." Zbigniew Brzezinski comments on the latter analogy: "One is tempted to add, they do not invade other countries, they only liberate."

In 1998, American political author, Charles A. Kupchan, described the world order "After Pax Americana" and projected: "America's military strength will remain as central to global stability in the years ahead as it has been in the past."

The Russian analyst Leonid Grinin argues that at present and in the nearest future *Pax Americana* will remain an effective tool for supporting the world order since the US concentrates too many leadership functions which no other country can take to the full extent. Thus, he warns that the destruction of *Pax Americana* will bring critical transformations of the World-system with unclear consequences.

American political analyst Ian Bremmer states that with the election of Donald Trump and the subsequent rise in populism in the west, as well as US withdrawal from international agreements such as the Trans-Pacific Partnership, NAFTA, and the Paris Climate Accords, the *Pax Americana* is over.

## Bibliography


"Axis Aggression." National Museum of American History, November 9, 2021. https://americanhistory.si.edu/price-of-freedom/world-war-ii/axis-aggression.

Goodman, Paul. "The 8 Main Reasons for War." Owlcation. Owlcation, October 6, 2014. https://owlcation.com/social-sciences/The-Main-Reasons-For-War.

"History of the UN Seventieth Anniversary." United Nations. United Nations. https://www.un.org/un70/en/content/history/index.html.

History.com Editors. "Marshall Plan." History.com. A&E Television Networks, December 16, 2009. https://www.history.com/topics/world-war-ii/marshall-plan-1.

Kent, Lenny, By, Lenny Kent, and Name *. "Why Is the U.S. Sending Troops to Kuwait?" About The Character, June 4, 2022. https://aboutthecharacter.com/qa/why-is-the-u-s-sending-troops-to-kuwait.html.

"Occupation and Continued Warfare." Encyclopædia Britannica. https://www.britannica.com/event/Iraq-War/Occupation-and-continued-warfare.

"Pax Americana." Wikipedia. Wikimedia Foundation, October 23, 2022. https://en.wikipedia.org/wiki/Pax_Americana.

"Project for the New American Century." Citizendium. https://en.citizendium.org/wiki/Project_for_the_New_American_Century.

U.S. Department of State. U.S. Department of State. https://history.state.gov/milestones/1899-1913/war.

"The U.S. in WWI - Overview." Home - World War I Centennial. https://www.worldwar1centennial.org/index.php/edu-home/edu-topics/579-overview-general-collections/4989-the-u-s-in-wwi-overview.html.

"United States–Latin American Relations." Encyclopedia.com. https://www.encyclopedia.com/humanities/encyclopedias-almanacs-transcripts-and-maps/united-states-latin-american-relations.

"War in Afghanistan (2001–2021)." Wikipedia. Wikimedia Foundation, October 28, 2022. https://en.wikipedia.org/wiki/War_in_Afghanistan_(2001%E2%80%932021).

"War of 1812 Overview." USS Constitution Museum, March 19, 2019. https://ussconstitutionmuseum.org/major-events/war-of-1812-overview/.

"Why Is the U.S. Sending Troops to Kuwait? - about the Character." https://aboutthecharacter.com/qa/why-is-the-u-s-sending-troops-to-kuwait.html.

# Chapter 4

# The Costs of American Militarism vs. Peace: Constructive Solutions

## The Costs of America's Wars

Let us attempt to document the direct and indirect human and financial costs of American wars versus using the money spent on these wars and avoiding the human, financial, and property losses instead of expending those resources for peaceful and humanitarian benefits.

The United States has invaded or fought in 84 of the 193 countries recognized by the United Nations and has been militarily involved with 191 of 193 – a staggering 98 percent. There are only three countries in the world that America hasn't invaded or has never seen a U.S. military presence: Andorra, Bhutan, and Liechtenstein.

Some general and more specific examples of the costs of American wars follow. Through the Spanish, English, Dutch, and French invasions and settlements in North America and the Caribbean from 1492 to 1900, it is estimated that Indigenous People genocides killed an estimated 12 million indigenous people through disease and war between 1492 and 1900.

In their most recent calculations, the Costs of War Project estimates that post-9/11 wars participated in by the US have exceeded $8 trillion in costs and directly killed 897,000 to 929,000 people in Iraq, Afghanistan, Pakistan, Syria, and Yemen. This figure includes $2.2 trillion reserved for veterans' care through 2050. A 2021 report from the project concluded that since September 11, 2001, four times more U.S. veterans and service members had died by suicide than had been killed in combat.

Let us examine the costs of the wars that we described in the previous chapter. According to the 'U.S. Congressional Research Service, Costs of U.S. Major Wars' report. Here is a summary of the actual military costs of American wars.

Here are additional notes on the costs of these wars.[60]

**War of 1812**

**Casualty statistics**:

| **USA** | **Great Britain** |
| --- | --- |
| Killed – 15,000 | Killed – 8600 |
| Wounded – 4,505 | Wounded -Unknown |

**War Cost**

[60] "Peace, But at What Cost?," Encyclopedia.com, https://www.encyclopedia.com/history/educational-magazines/peace-what-cost.

**For United States**

| Years of War | Year of War<br>Current Year |
| --- | --- |
| 1812-1815 | $158 million<br>$3.166 Trillion |

**USA gains from war**

The War of 1812 changed the course of American history. Because America had managed to fight the world's greatest military power to a virtual standstill, it **gained international respect**. Furthermore, it instilled a greater sense of nationalism among its citizens.

**Mexican American War 1846 – 1848**

**Casualty statistics**

| USA | Mexican |
| --- | --- |
| Killed – 1733 | Killed – Approx. 5,000 |
| Wounded - 4,152 | Wounded - Unknown |

**War Costs**

**USA**

The war cost the United States $71 million, the 11th-most expensive war in U.S. history. Military Costs in 2022: $2.665 trillion

**Mexico**

The country spent $100 million to finance the war.

**USA gains from war:**

Under the Treaty of Guadalupe Hidalgo, which settled the Mexican-American War, the United States gained more than 500,000 square miles (1,300,000 square km) of land, expanding U.S. territory by about one-third.

## Spanish American War: April 10, 1898 – December 10, 1898

**Casualty statistics**:

| **USA** | **Spain** |
| --- | --- |
| Killed – 3,289 | Killed – Approx. 60,000 |
| Wounded - 2,061 | Wounded – Unknown |

**War Cost**

**United States**

| **Year of war** | **Current Year** |
| --- | --- |
| $250 million | $8.921 Trillion |

**USA Gains from War**

Representatives of Spain and the United States signed a peace treaty in Paris on December 10, 1898, which established the independence of Cuba, ceded Puerto Rico and Guam to the United States, and allowed the victorious power to purchase the Philippines Islands from Spain for $20 million. The United States acquired Puerto

Rico, Guam, and the Philippines as territories. The United States also annexed the independent state of Hawaii during the conflict.

**Philippines-America War: 1899 – 1902**

**Casualty statistics**:

| **USA** | **Philippines** |
|---|---|
| Killed –4200 | Killed – Approx. 200,000 |
| Wounded - 2,900 | Wounded - Thousands wounded |

**War Cost**

**United States**

| **Years of war** | **Current Year** |
|---|---|
| $400 million | $14.103 Trillion |

**USA Gains from War**

Through its victory, the United States gained a strategically located colonial base for its commercial and military interests in the Asian-Pacific region.

## World War I 1914 – 1918 [61]

---

[61] "Costs of Major Us Wars," Naval History and Heritage Command, https://www.history.navy.mil/research/library/online-reading-room/title-list-alphabetically/c/costs-major-us-wars.html.

**Casualties and Losses**

**Casualty statistics**:

| **Entente Powers** | **Total number of dead** |
|---|---|
| United States of America | 117,000 |
| Great Britain and Ireland | 1,350,000 |
| Belgium | 88,000 |
| France | 1,927,000 |
| Greece | 25,000 |
| Italy | 1,160,000 |
| Japan | 1,000 |
| Montenegro | 13,000 |
| Portugal | 7,000 |
| Romania | 550,000 |
| Russia | 2,311,000 to |
| | 2,754,369 |
| Serbia | 525,000 |
| Australia | 61,966 |
| New Zealand | 18,052 |
| **Central Powers** | **Total number of dead** |
| Austro-Hungarian Empire | 1,860,000 |
| Bulgaria | 388,000 |
| Germany | 2,737000 |
| Turkey | 232,000 |

**War Cost**

**United States**

| **Year of War** | **Current Year** |
|---|---|
| $32 billion | $6.276 Trillion |

**Allies**

| **Year of war** | **Current Year** |
|---|---|
| $147 billion | $2.833 Quadrillion |

**Central Powers**

| **Year of war** | **Current Year** |
|---|---|
| $61 billion | $1.996 Trillion |

**USA gains from World War I**

While World War I redrew political borders and introduced modern weaponry such as poison gas, machine guns, and tanks. In addition, the conflict heralded the rise in America of conscription, mass propaganda, the national security state, and the FBI. It accelerated income tax and urbanization and helped make America the pre-eminent economic and military power in the world. By the end of World War I, the United States produced more goods and services than any other nation, both in total and per person. Americans had more steel, food, cloth, and coal than even the richest foreign nations combined.

# World War II 1939 – 1945[62]

## Casualties and Losses

**Casualty statistics**:

| DEATHS BY COUNTRY | |
|---|---|
| **Country** | **Total Civilian and Military Deaths** |
| United States | 418,500 |
| Albania | 30,200 |
| Australia | 40,500 |
| Austria | 3,84,700 |
| Belgium | 86,100 |
| Brazil | 2,000 |
| Bulgaria | 25,000 |
| Canada | 45,400 |
| China | 35,000,000 |
| Czechoslovakia | 345,000 |
| Denmark | 3,200 |
| Dutch East Indies | 400,000 |
| Estonia | 51,000 |
| Ethiopia | 100,000 |
| Finland | 97,000 |
| France | 567,600 |
| French Indochina | 1,500,000 |

[62] "Costs of Major Us Wars," Naval History and Heritage Command, https://www.history.navy.mil/research/library/online-reading-room/title-list-alphabetically/c/costs-major-us-wars.html.

| DEATHS BY COUNTRY | |
|---|---|
| **Country** | **Total Civilian and Military Deaths** |
| Germany | 6,600,000-8,800,000 |
| Greece | 300,000-800,000 |
| Hungary | 580,000 |
| India | 1,500,000-2,500,000 |
| Italy | 4,57,000 |
| Japan | 2,600,000-3,100,000 |
| Korea | 378,000-473,000 |
| Latvia | 227,000 |
| Lithuania | 353,000 |
| Luxembourg | 2,000 |
| Malaya | 100,000 |
| Netherlands | 301,000 |
| New Zealand | 11,900 |
| Norway | 9,500 |
| Papua New Guinea | 15,000 |
| Philippines | 500,000-1,000,000 |
| Poland | 560,000 |
| Romania | 833,000 |
| Singapore | 50,000 |
| South Africa | 11,900 |
| Soviet Union | 23,400,000 |
| United Kingdom | 450,700 |
| Yugoslavia | 10,000 |

**WORLDWIDE CASUALTIES (Approx.)**

| | |
|---|---|
| Battle Deaths | 15,000,000 |
| Battle Wounded | 25,000,000 |
| Civilian Deaths | 45,000,000 |

**War II Costs**

| Country | Billions USD | 2022 Cost |
|---|---|---|
| United States of America | $ 341.491 | $5,618 Trillion |
| Germany | $ 270.000 | $.4.443 Trillion |
| Soviet Union | $ 192.000 | $.3160 Trillion |
| China | $ 190.000 | $3.127 Trillion |
| United Kingdom | $ 120.000 | $1.97 Trillion |
| Canada | $ 15.680 | $257.00 Billion |
| Italy | $ 94.000 | $154.667 Billion |
| Japan | $ 56.000 | $92.142 Billion |
| France | $ 15.000 | $246.80 Billion |
| Belgium | $ 3.250 | $53.47 Billion |
| Poland | $ 1.550 | $24.68 Billion |
| **Total** | **$ 1.301 trillion** | **$18.929 trillion** |

## Korean War 1950 – 1953

**Casualties and Losses**

**Killed:**

| USA | South Korea | North Korea | UN | China |
|---|---|---|---|---|
| 54,246 | 137,889 | 520,000 | 40,670 | 115,786 |
| **Wounded**: | | | | |
| 112,000 | 450,742 | 120,000 | 104,280 | 222,000 |

**War Cost**

**For United States:**

| Year of War | Current Year |
|---|---|
| $30 Billion | $366.667 Trillion |

**USA gains from war**

The impact of the Korean War on the Economy of the United States refers to the ways in which the American economy was affected by the Korean experience from 1950 to 1953. The Korean War boosted GDP growth through government spending, which in turn constrained investment and consumption.

## Vietnam War 1964 – 1975

**Casualties and Losses:**

| USA | North and South Vietnam |
|---|---|
| Killed – 58,000 | 1,100,000 |

**War Cost**

**For United States:**

| **Year of War** | **Current Year** |
|---|---|
| **$168 Billion** | **$9.249 Trillion** |

**USA gains from war**

The Vietnam War severely damaged the U.S. economy. Unwilling to raise taxes to pay for the war, President Johnson unleashed a cycle of inflation. The war also weakened U.S. military morale and undermined, for a time, the U.S. commitment to internationalism.

## Gulf War War I (1990 – 1991)

## Gulf War II (and Occupation): 2003 – 2020

**Casualties and losses**

| **USA** | **Iraq** |
|---|---|
| Killed: 4,825 | Killed: 800,000 (approx.) |

**War Cost**

**For the United States:**

| **Year of War** | **Current Year** |
|---|---|
| $2.43 Trillion | $3.913 Trillion |

**Cost of Reconstruction:**

| **Years of occupation** | **Current Year** |
|---|---|
| $144 Billion | $228 Billion |

## Afghan War: 2001 – 2021

**Casualty statistics**:

| **USA** | **Afghanistan** |
|---|---|
| Killed: 2,456 | Killed – 243,000 |

**War Cost**

**For United States**

| **Years of War** | **Year of War**<br>**Current Year** |
|---|---|
| 2001-2021 | $2.313 Trillion<br>$ 3.86 Trillion |

**Cost of Reconstruction (since 2003):** $144 Billion
**Current Year:** $2.317 Trillion

## Cost of the Marshall Plan

$13 Billion (1945) to $2.371 Trillion (2022)

Cost of US reconstruction of post-war Japan: Between 1946 and 1952, Washington invested $2.2 billion — or $18 billion in real 21st-century dollars adjusted for inflation — in Japan's reconstruction effort.

## Defense Spending by Country 2022[63]

| Country | 2020 Spending | 2019 Spending | % GDP 2020 |
|---|---|---|---|
| United States | $766.58 Bn | $734.34 Bn | 3.70% |
| China | $244.93 Bn | $240.33 Bn | 1.70% |
| India | $73.00 Bn | $71.47 Bn | 2.90% |
| Russia | $66.84 Bn | $65.20 Bn | 4.30% |
| Saudi Arabia | $55.53 Bn | $61.95 Bn | 8.40% |
| United Kingdom | $58.48 Bn | $56.86 Bn | 2.20% |
| France | $51.57 Bn | $50.12 Bn | 2.10% |
| Germany | $51.57 Bn | $49.01 Bn | 1.40% |
| Japan | $48.16 Bn | $47.61 Bn | 1.00% |
| South Korea | $46.06 Bn | $43.89 Bn | 2.80% |
| Italy | $28.37 Bn | $26.38 Bn | 1.60% |
| Australia | $27.62 Bn | $26.08 Bn | 2.10% |
| Brazil | $25.10 Bn | $25.91 Bn | 1.40% |
| Canada | $22.85 Bn | $22.20 Bn | 1.40% |
| Turkey | $19.57 Bn | $20.60 Bn | 2.80% |

63 "Defense Spending by Country 2022," https://worldpopulationreview.com/country-rankings/defense-spending-by-country.

| Country | 2020 Spending | 2019 Spending | % GDP 2020 |
|---|---|---|---|
| Israel | $21.07 Bn | $20.50 Bn | 5.60% |
| Spain | $17.16 Bn | $17.19 Bn | 1.40% |
| Iran | $12.15 Bn | $12.53 Bn | 2.20% |
| Netherlands | $12.21 Bn | $12.00 Bn | 1.40% |
| Poland | $12.81 Bn | $11.79 Bn | 2.20% |
| Singapore | $11.02 Bn | $10.66 Bn | 3.20% |
| Pakistan | $10.10 Bn | $10.39 Bn | 4.00% |
| Algeria | $9.96 Bn | $10.30 Bn | 6.70% |
| Colombia | $10.13 Bn | $10.17 Bn | 3.40% |
| Indonesia | $9.49 Bn | $9.00 Bn | 0.90% |
| Iraq | $6.99 Bn | $7.60 Bn | 4.10% |
| Norway | $7.51 Bn | $7.52 Bn | 1.90% |
| Kuwait | $6.94 Bn | $7.37 Bn | 6.50% |
| Thailand | $7.36 Bn | $7.29 Bn | 1.50% |
| Mexico | $6.61 Bn | $6.65 Bn | 0.60% |
| Oman | $6.66 Bn | $6.55 Bn | 10.90% |
| Sweden | $6.23 Bn | $5.84 Bn | 1.20% |
| Greece | $5.24 Bn | $5.47 Bn | 2.80% |
| Ukraine | $6.00 Bn | $5.42 Bn | 4.10% |
| Chile | $5.04 Bn | $5.18 Bn | 1.90% |
| Switzerland | $5.43 Bn | $5.11 Bn | 0.80% |
| Belgium | $5.33 Bn | $4.76 Bn | 1.10% |
| Romania | $5.58 Bn | $4.61 Bn | 2.30% |
| Denmark | $4.84 Bn | $4.56 Bn | 1.40% |
| Bangladesh | $4.33 Bn | $4.35 Bn | 1.30% |

## Why Does America Invest So Heavily in Its Military?

Is America's investment in its military the biggest in the world? Let's examine the chart below. Yes, in terms of actual spending, the U.S. spends more than any other nation on earth. As a percentage of the world nations' GDP, we see from the chart below that America ranks #9 in the percentage.

The question here is: Does America use this huge amount of money for peaceful or military purposes? Since the withdrawal of U.S. forces from Afghanistan and Iraq, where has the "peace dividend" gone is also a good question. The U.S. now maintains and controls about 750 bases in at least 80 countries worldwide. Is there an American empire that the U.S. seeks to uphold as the great historical empires of ancient and modern times from biblical days to the Greeks, Romans, Ottomans, or the British? Most military analysts and historians will say that since World War II, the United States has relied on a global network of military bases and forces to protect its interests and allies. But the international environment has changed dramatically over the decades, and economic concerns have risen, leading some to debate just what America's role should now be in the world.

American policymakers' choice of the current U.S. home and overseas military spending depends on an assessment of how the United States can help achieve its global security interests. Perspectives on the role of the American military in achieving U.S. global security interests differ.

Reducing U.S. military spending does not make sense if one's perspective is that a global American military presence plays a vital role in deterring and responding to perceived threats. Relying more on allies could lead to reductions in U.S. military spending. The role of the United States and its global military presence is under constant legislative debate due to the huge expense required from the American taxpayer for that huge military posture. Most Americans do not want to pay for the U.S. to play the role of the "world's policeman," but they also know the costs and dangers of isolationism historically.

It is time for U.S. policymakers to address the critical strategic choices on what role the American military presence and spending can play in achieving U.S. global security interests such as protecting itself, its allies, and global trade. Also, policymakers need to address the question of what other non-military methods are available for the U.S. to achieve its global interests. Perhaps a good example for Americans to consider is the Chinese 'Belt and Road Initiative', which seeks to help developing countries and is a good way to make a better world for the human beings.

The ultimate question arises: Would America's international defense strategy be better served by equalizing the two expenses of military spending and international development aid?

## America Foreign Aid Expenditures Comparison

Let us now compare the amounts of financial aid that various nations provide globally in the below chart. The chart reveals that though the U.S. is the second largest international development aid donor at $34.6 Billion yearly, that amount represents only .16% of its GDP. By comparison, the U.S. defense spending is 3.60% of its GDP. By further comparison, note here that China is the largest international development aid donor at $38 Billion yearly, and that amount represents .36% of its GDP.

### List of Development Aid Country Donors 2021

International development aid is given by many non-private donors. The first table is based on official development assistance (ODA) figures published by the OECD for members of its Development Assistance Committee (DAC). Non-DAC members included in the OECD's publishing are listed separately.

Development Assistance by DAC Members

| Donor | Total development aid | Development aid per capita | % of GDP |
|---|---|---|---|
| Australia | $2.95 billion | $129.92 | 0.22 |
| Austria | $1.21 billion | $137.59 | 0.27 |
| Belgium | $2.18 billion | $167.20 | 0.42 |
| Canada | $6.4 billion | $170.25 | 0.27 |
| Czech Republic | $310 million | $18.85 | 0.13 |
| Denmark | $2.55 billion | $447.05 | 0.71 |
| EU Institutions (excl. EU members) | $14.827 billion | $27.03 | |
| Finland | $1.13 billion | $234.13 | 0.42 |

| Donor | Total development aid | Development aid per capita | % of GDP |
|---|---|---|---|
| France | $12.18 billion | $137.35 | 0.44 |
| Germany | $23.81 billion | $214.73 | 0.60 |
| Greece | $310 million | $25.04 | 0.14 |
| Iceland | $70 million | $120.29 | 0.27 |
| Ireland | $940 million | $151.2 | 0.31 |
| Italy | $4.9 billion | $63.38 | 0.24 |
| Japan | $15.51 billion | $73.58 | 0.29 |
| Luxembourg | $470 million | $609.48 | 1.05 |
| Netherlands | $5.29 billion | $338.38 | 0.59 |
| New Zealand | $560 million | $90.75 | 0.28 |
| Norway | $4.29 billion | $812.58 | 1.02 |
| Poland | $680 million | $11.45 | 0.12 |
| Portugal | $370 million | $30.07 | 0.16 |
| Slovak Republic | $130 million | $16.56 | 0.12 |
| Slovenia | $90 million | $29.04 | 0.16 |
| South Korea | $2.52 billion | $37.13 | 0.15 |
| Spain | $2.90 billion | $34.52 | 0.21 |
| Sweden | $5.40 billion | $701.10 | 0.99 |
| Switzerland | $3.09 billion | $421.37 | 0.44 |

| Donor | Total development aid | Development aid per capita | % of GDP |
|---|---|---|---|
| United Kingdom | $19.37 billion | $284.85 | 0.50 |
| United States | $34.62 billion | $95.52 | 0.16 |

## Development Assistance by Non-DAC Members

Non-DAC members reported the following figures:

| Donor | Total development aid | Development aid per capita | % of GNI |
|---|---|---|---|
| China | $38 billion | $27.86 | 0.36 |
| UAE | $12.24 billion | $467 | 0.55 |
| Turkey | $8.652 billion | $47 | 1.15 |
| Qatar | $2 billion | $757.80 | 1.17 |
| Russia | $1.14 billion | $8 | 0.03 |
| India | $2.4 billion | $21.24 | 0.65 |
| Israel | $280 million | $24 | 0.07 |
| Hungary | $150 million | $15 | 0.1 |
| Lithuania | $60 million | $14 | 0.11 |
| Croatia | $50 million | $12 | 0.14 |
| Estonia | $40 million | $23 | 0.13 |
| Malta | $40 million | $22 | 0.3 |

| Donor | Total development aid | Development aid per capita | % of GNI |
|---|---|---|---|
| Latvia | $30 million | $10 | 0.10 |

## World Bank and International Monetary Fund

Here we should discuss the World Bank Group and how it works with developing countries to reduce poverty and increase shared prosperity, and the International Monetary Fund serves to stabilize the international monetary system and acts as a monitor of the world's currencies.

The International Monetary Fund (IMF), and its affiliate the World Bank, is a major financial agency of the United Nations, and an international financial institution, headquartered in Washington, D.C., consisting of 190 countries. Its stated mission is "working to foster global monetary cooperation, secure financial stability, facilitate international trade, promote high employment and sustainable economic growth, and reduce poverty around the world."

The Bretton Woods Conference, officially known as the United Nations Monetary and Financial Conference, was a gathering of delegates from 44 nations that met from July 1 to 22, 1944, in Bretton Woods, New Hampshire, United States in order to agree upon a series of new rules for the post-WWII international monetary system. The two major accomplishments of the conference were the creation of the International Monetary Fund (IMF) and the International Bank for Reconstruction and Development (IBRD).

The lessons taken by U.S. policymakers from the interwar period informed the institutions created at the conference. Based on the economic ideas of Americans Harry Dexter White and John Maynard Keynes, American officials such as President Franklin D. Roosevelt and Secretary of State Cordell Hull were adherents of the Wilsonian belief that free trade not only promoted international prosperity but also international peace. The experience of the 1930s certainly suggested as much. The policies adopted by governments to combat the Great Depression - high tariff barriers, competitive currency devaluations, discriminatory trading blocs - had created an unstable international environment without improving the economic situation. This experience led international leaders to conclude that economic cooperation was the only way to achieve both peace and prosperity, at home and abroad.

IMF funds come from three sources: member quotas and multilateral and bilateral borrowing agreements. Countries with larger quotas, and thus larger financial commitments to the institution, have a greater say in how the IMF is run. The United States is the largest contributor; see the listing below of contributions to the IMF by the top donors:

- U.S. Dollar: US$5,052.94 billion
- Euro: US$1,559.26 billion
- Chinese Yuan: US$84.51 billion
- Japanese Yen: US$332.77 billion
- British Pound: US$349.33 billion

The currency composition of the SDR basket is reviewed every five years. The current weights for the component currencies are as follows:

- U.S. Dollar: 41.73%
- Euro: 30.93%
- Chinese Yuan: 10.92%
- Japanese Yen: 8.33%
- British Pound: 8.09%

The question here is if development funding could be increased by all lenders—American, Chinese, Asian, or European—would that activity be more conducive to world peace than increasing military budgets by these nationalist blocks?

## America: The World's Policeman or Bully?

Obviously, it is almost incomprehensible to try and contemplate the massive loss of lives that wars have caused throughout history, as well as the economic losses. The idea that America is the world's modern-day policeman has been debated fiercely within the United States and internationally. America did not start World War I and World War II. America did not have to fund the Marshall Plan in Europe and Japan. Nor is America required to be the largest donor and lender of foreign development funds in the world.

There are many questions and judgments that come up in hindsight when reviewing the militaristic nature of the United States. Should

America have remained isolationist in those wars? What were the choices? If the German Kaiser's armies had won Europe, what would the consequences be for the United States? If Hitler had won Europe and been allowed to continue the development in Germany of the atomic bomb, what would be the consequences not only for America but also for Asia, Africa, and Latin America? If America had not bombed Hiroshima and Nagasaki, how many more American and Japanese soldiers and Japanese citizens would have died?

Of course, in considering other conflicts like Vietnam, Afghanistan, and Iraq, plus all the historical covert CIA operations that were initiated and horribly executed by the U.S. military, can we say indeed that America is a bully?

While this question can be debated endlessly, we feel it is much more constructive to imagine a truly just and peaceful world society. Because of America's great influence in the world, it is useful to examine America's endemic problems and discuss how to fix them and the costs of fixing them versus the costs of American militarism.

# America's 15 Main Problems and Their Costs[64]

What are the most important issues Americans think need to be fixed, as polled by the prestigious Pew Research Group, 2021 follows here.

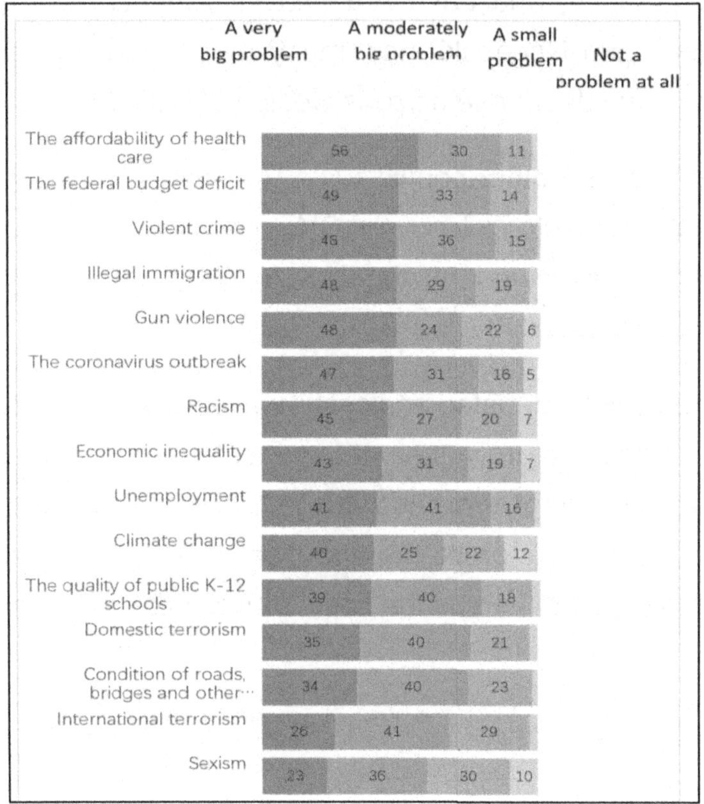


"Americans' Views of the Problems Facing the Nation," Pew Research Center - U.S. Politics & Policy (Pew Research Center, July 25, 2022), https://www.pewresearch.org/politics/2021/04/15/americans-views-of-the-problems-facing-the-nation/.

## #1 The Affordability of Health Care

Many U.S. adults have trouble affording health care costs. While lower-income and uninsured adults are the most likely to report this, those with health insurance and those with higher incomes are not immune to the high cost of medical care. About half of U.S. adults say that it is very or somewhat difficult for them to afford their health care costs (47%). Among those under age 65, uninsured adults are much more likely to say affording health care costs is difficult (85%) compared to those with health insurance coverage (47%). Additionally, at least six in ten Black adults (60%) and Hispanic adults (65%) report difficulty affording health care costs compared to about four in ten White adults (39%). Adults in households with annual incomes under $40,000 are more than three times as likely as adults in households with incomes over $90,000 to say it is difficult to afford their health care costs (69% v. 21%).

**Cost**: (Amount of money estimated to fix the problem - Health care costs totaled over $90 billion or about 2.5% of health care spending)

(Source: https://www.prnewswire.com/news-releases/yearly-cost-of-crime-in-us-2-6-trillion-first-estimate-in-25-years-301230849.html)

## #2 The Federal Budget Deficit

The Congressional Budget Office estimates that the federal government ran a deficit of $217 billion in August 2022, the eleventh month of FY2022. This deficit was the difference between $304 billion in revenues and $521 billion in spending. The U.S. is the largest debtor nation in the world, with debt at 104% of GDP.

Large tax cuts passed by Congress during the presidencies of George W. Bush and Donald Trump have played a large part in the subsequent deterioration of government finances and the resulting growth in the national debt.

As of August, 2022, it costs $677.6 billion to maintain the debt just in interest payments, which is 12.66% of the total Federal spending. The national debt has increased every year over the past ten years. Servicing deficits (and the debt) takes away spending money to solve America's other problems.

**Cost:** (Amount of money estimated to fix the problem) In FY 2021, total U.S. government spending was $6.82 trillion, and total revenue was $4.05 trillion, resulting in a deficit of $2.77 trillion, a decrease of $359.74 billion from the previous fiscal year.) Website URL below: (https://fiscaldata.treasury.gov/americas-finance-guide/national-deficit)

## #3 Violent Crime

There were an estimated 366.7 violent crimes per 100,000 inhabitants in 2019, a rate that dropped 1.0 percent when compared with the 2018 estimated violent crime rate and fell 9.3 percent from the 2010 estimate.

In 2016, the FBI Director approved the recommendation to discontinue reporting rape data using the UCR legacy definition beginning in 2017. However, to maintain the 20-year trend, the rape total for the legacy definition is used to calculate the violent crime total.

Aggravated assaults accounted for 68.2 percent of violent crimes reported to law enforcement in 2019. Robbery offenses accounted for 22.3 percent of violent crime offenses; rape (legacy definition) accounted for 8.2 percent, and murder accounted for 1.4 percent.

**Cost** (Amount of money estimated to fix the problem- Costs of violent crime are dominated by wages and housework ... Overall, personal crime in the U.S. cost *almost $2.6 trillion in 2017.)*

*(*Source: https://www.prnewswire.com/news-releases/yearly-cost-of-crime-in-us-2-6-trillion-first-estimate-in-25-years-301230849.html)

## #4 Illegal Immigration

This report presents estimates of the US undocumented population for 2017 derived by the Center for Migration Studies of New York (CMS). It focuses on the steep decline in the undocumented population from Mexico since 2010. While the president has focused the nation's attention on the border wall, *half a million* US undocumented residents from Mexico left the undocumented population in 2020 alone, more than three times the number that arrived that year. Today the number of illegal aliens entering the country every year is recorded as 2,701,000 persons.

**Cost:** (Amount of money estimated to fix the problem- Illegal immigration costs $275 billion a year.)

(Source: https://www.nbcnews.com/politics/donald-trump/fact-check-how-much-does-illegal-immigration-cost-america-not-n950981)

## #5 Gun violence

Gun violence is a contemporary global human rights issue. Gun-related violence threatens our most fundamental human right, the right to life.

When people are afraid of gun violence, this can also have a negative impact on people's right to education or health care when they are too afraid to attend schools or health facilities or if these services are not fully functioning due to firearm violence in their community.

Gun violence in the United States results in tens of thousands of deaths and injuries annually and was the leading cause of death for children 19 and younger in 2020. In 2018, the most recent year for which data are available as of 2021, the Centers for Disease Control and Prevention's (CDC) National Center for Health Statistics reports 38,390 deaths by firearm, of which 24,432 were by suicide. The rate of firearm deaths per 100,000 people rose from 10.3 per 100,000 in 1999 to 12 per 100,000 in 2017, with 109 people dying per day or about 14,542 homicides in total being 11.9 per 100,000 in 2018. In 2010, there were 19,392 firearm-related suicides, and 11,078 firearm-related homicides in the U.S. In 2010, 358 murders were reported involving a rifle while 6,009 were reported involving a handgun; another 1,939 were reported with an unspecified type of firearm. In 2020, a total of 45,200 fatal and nonfatal violent crimes were committed with a firearm, or approximately 124 people per day.

**Cost**: (Amount of money estimated to fix the problem- Governments are spending a combined average of nearly $35 million each day to deal with the aftermath of gun violence across the country)

(Source: https://everytownresearch.org/report/the-economic-cost-of-gun-violence/)

## #6 The Coronavirus Outbreak

The United States officially surpassed one million reported COVID-19 deaths on May 16, 2022, according to data from the John Hopkins Coronavirus Resource Center.

It's a morbid milestone for a virus that claimed its first American lives in early 2020, and rapidly became the third leading cause of U.S. deaths.

President Biden marked what he called the "tragic milestone" on May 12, 2022, by ordering all flags flown at half-staff and demanding that citizens "remain vigilant against this pandemic" that has infected nearly 60% of the U.S. population.

Data from the Centers for Disease Control and Prevention indicated that the emergence of COVID-19 as the third leading cause of U.S. deaths after heart disease and cancer in 2020 and 2021 also lowered life expectancy in both years.

Many deaths in the United States and worldwide could have been averted if more people had received vaccines. Just two-thirds of the total U.S. population has been fully vaccinated, according to CRC data. And 40% of the global population, approximately 3 billion people, remains unvaccinated.

Cost: (The US spent $5 trillion to fight the pandemic. But how to calculate the value of a million American lives?)

(Source:https://coronavirus.jhu.edu/from-our-experts/u-s-officially-surpasses-1-million-covid-19-deaths)

## #7 Racism

Girls and gender-nonconforming youth of color are cultural influencers and leaders, reshaping our world with their passion, ingenuity, activism, and joy. Yet, they are chronically mis- and underrepresented in mainstream media, and they are often not taken seriously as agents of culture.

Racism has manifested itself in various ways, including genocide, slavery, lynchings, segregation, Native American reservations and boarding schools, racist immigration and naturalization laws, and internment camps. Formal racial discrimination was largely banned by the mid-20th century and, over time, came to be perceived as being socially and morally unacceptable. Racial politics remains a major phenomenon, and racism continues to be reflected in socioeconomic inequality. Into the 21st century, research has uncovered extensive evidence of racial discrimination in various sectors of modern U.S. society, including the criminal justice system, business, the economy, housing, health care, the media, and politics. According to the United Nations and the U.S. Human Rights Network, "discrimination in the United States permeates all aspects of life and extends to all communities of color."

**Cost:** (Amount of money estimated to fix the problem) U.S. economy lost $16 Trillion because of discrimination.

(Source: https://www.npr.org/sections/live-updates-protests-for-racial-justice/2020/09/23/916022472/cost-of-racism-u-s-economy-lost-16-trillion-because-of-discrimination-bank-says)

## #8 Economic Inequality

Income inequality has long been a political and economic hot topic in the United States. As of 2021, the richest 10% of Americans owned almost 70% of the wealth in the country, while the poorest 50% owned around 2.5%—a staggering gap that has widened substantially in the last several decades. In 2020, 11.4% of the country's population (or 37.2 million individuals) lived in poverty. Technology, globalization, and educational deficiency fail to explain how the wealthy were able to reshape the U.S. economy into a winner-take-all system that, in a distributive sense, resembles more closely the oligarchic systems of Mexico, Brazil, and Russia than the economies of other Western democracies.

**Cost** (Amount of money estimated to fix the problem - Inequality in employment, education and earnings has cost the U.S. economy nearly $22.9 trillion over the past 30 years.)

(Source: https://www.bloomberg.com/news/articles/2021-09-09/inequality-cost-u-s-nearly-23-trillion-since-)

## #9 Unemployment

The European roots of the United States come from nations with significant disparity between a small ruling class and the masses, where poverty was typical. Severing political connections to Great Britain, the 1776 Declaration of Independence aspired for equality, although the systems that were created replicated many old patterns. European settlers imagined a boundless wilderness to tame in America and created disparity with indigenous populations. The Industrial Revolution of the mid-1800s followed patterns established by military organizations originally meant to serve the interests of kings and queens. Schools were built to serve agriculture and new industrial enterprises. Today, these systems still resemble early efforts to create a conforming labor pool.

The economy that was first installed in the United States did not produce a middle class. The growth of a middle class came from the Homestead Act of 1862 and the Morrill Land-Grant Act of 1862, which made land available for farms and schools; the creation of the Federal Deposit Insurance Corp. that made banking secure for citizens in 1933; the establishment of the Federal Housing Administration in 1934 that made the home buying financially safe;

the labor policies of the mid-1930s and the Social Security Act of 1935 that provided an array of new benefits and protections to workers; the 1944 GI bill that gave grants to millions of veterans to attend college; and the Pell Grants of 1965 that made it possible for even more people to attend college. These policies produced a strong middle class. In the 1980s, principles of free market enterprise influenced economic development. Financial crises in the 2000s led to a major recession and job losses, costing billions of extra federal aid to America. In recent decades, many policymakers have become concerned about a middle class that is shrinking. To reduce poverty rates, transformational leaders can advocate for employment and equal pay policies that serve most Americans.

**Cost**: (Amount of money estimated to fix the problem - States issued $794 billion in combined state and federal unemployment benefits from March 2020 through July 2021)

(Source: https://www.cnbc.com/2021/09/02/pandemics-794-billion-unemployment-benefits-were-historic-heres-why.html)

## #10 Climate Change

Causes of Climate Change. Generating electricity and heat by burning fossil fuels causes a large chunk of global emissions. Most electricity is still generated by burning coal, oil, or gas, which produces carbon dioxide and nitrous oxide – powerful greenhouse gases that blanket the Earth and trap the sun's heat.

Climate change is changing water availability, making it scarcer in more regions. Global warming exacerbates water shortages in already water-stressed regions and is leading to an increased risk of agricultural droughts affecting crops and ecological droughts increasing the vulnerability of ecosystems. Droughts can also stir destructive sand and dust storms that can move billions of tons of sand across continents. Deserts are expanding, reducing land for growing food. Many people now face the threat of not having enough water regularly.

Climate change increases the factors that put and keep people in poverty. Floods may sweep away urban slums, destroying homes and livelihoods. Heat can make it difficult to work in outdoor jobs. Water scarcity may affect crops. Over the past decade (2010–2019), weather-related events displaced an estimated 23.1 million people annually, leaving much more vulnerable to poverty. Most refugees come from countries that are most vulnerable and least ready to adapt to the impacts of climate change.

**Cost**: (Amount of money estimated to fix the problem -The President's Budget for the fiscal year 2023 invests $44.9 billion to tackle the climate crisis, an increase of nearly 60 percent over FY 2021.)

(Source: https://www.whitehouse.gov/omb/briefing-room/2022/04/04/quantifying-risks-to-the-federal-budget-from-climate-)

## #11 The Quality of Public K-12 Schools

Education in the United States is provided in public and private schools and by individuals through homeschooling. State governments set overall educational standards, often mandate standardized tests for K–12 public school systems and supervise, usually through a board of regents, state colleges, and universities. The bulk of the $1.3 trillion in funding comes from state and local governments, with federal funding accounts for only about $200 billion. Private schools are free to determine their own curriculum and staffing policies, with voluntary accreditation available through independent regional accreditation authorities, although some state regulations can apply.

The United States spends more per student on education than any other country. In 2020, the Economist Intelligence Unit rated U.S. education as the 14th best in the world. The Program for International Student Assessment coordinated by the OECD currently ranks the overall knowledge and skills of American 15-year-olds as 31st in the world in reading literacy, mathematics, and science with the average American student scoring 487.7, compared with the OECD average of 493. In 2020, the country spent 6.2% of its GDP on all levels of education – 1.0 percentage points above the OECD average of 5.2%. In 2020, 46.4% of Americans aged 25 to 64 attained some form of post-secondary education. 48% of Americans aged 25 to 34 attained some form of tertiary education, about 4% above the OECD average of 44%. 35% of Americans aged 25 and over have achieved a bachelor's degree or higher. The United States ranks 3rd from the bottom among OECD nations in terms of its poverty gap, and 4th from the bottom in terms of the poverty rate.

**Cost**: (Amount of money estimated to fix the problem) In addition to the $1.3 trillion from local & state funding, K-12 public schools spend $13,185 per pupil., Public K-12 expenditures total $666.9 billion.

(Source: https://educationdata.org/public-education-spending-statistics#:~:text=K%2D12%20public%20schools%20spend,to%203.41%25%20of)

## #12 Domestic Terrorism

In the United States, a common definition of terrorism is the systematic or threatened use of violence to create a general climate of fear to intimidate a population or government and thereby effect political, religious, or ideological change. There are numerous attempts to commit acts of terrorism, and other such items which pertain to terrorist activities which are engaged in by non-state actors or spies who are acting in the interests of state actors or persons who are acting without the approval of foreign governments within the domestic borders of the United States.

A June 2020 study of domestic terrorist incidents by the Center for Strategic and International Studies (CSIS) reported that during the previous 25 years, the majority of attacks and plots were perpetrated and hatched by far-right domestic attackers. This trend has accelerated in recent years, with this sector being responsible for about 66% of all of the attacks and plots which were perpetrated in 2019, and it was also responsible for 90% of all of those attacks which were perpetrated in 2020. The next most potentially dangerous group has been “religious extremists," the majority “Salafi jihadists inspired by the Islamic State and al-Qaeda." In contrast, the number planned by far left has reduced to a minute fraction since the mid-2000s.

**Cost** - (Amount of money estimated to fix the problem) The Department of Homeland Security FY 2022 President's Budget request includes $101.2 billion in investments to counter Domestic Terrorism (DT).

(Source: https://www.justice.gov/jmd/page/file/1398831/download)

## #13 Condition of Roads, Bridges, and Other Infrastructure

The World Economic Forum now ranks the United States 13th regarding the overall quality of infrastructure. Examples of our nation's fragile and aging infrastructure abound. More than 45,000 U.S. bridges and 1 in 5 miles of roads are in poor condition, per the American Society of Civil Engineers.

The American Society of Civil Engineers (ASCE) has compiled regular "report cards" on the state of U.S. infrastructure since the 1980s. In its 2021 report [PDF], the ASCE found that the nation's infrastructure averaged a "C-," up from a "D+" in 2017 and the highest grade in twenty years. Still, the group estimated that there is an "infrastructure investment gap" of nearly $2.6 trillion this decade that, if unaddressed, could cost the United States $10 trillion in lost GDP by 2039.

U.S. infrastructure performance suffers from its comparatively low quality, with consequences for businesses, workers, and travellers. U.S. passenger trains average just half the speed of Europe's high-speed rails. Aviation industry rankings cited by Business Roundtable put only four U.S. airports in the top fifty worldwide, with the top-ranked coming in at number thirty.

Cost: (Amount of money estimated to fix the problem) The $20 trillion U.S. economy relies on a vast infrastructure network from roads and bridges to freight rail and ports. Recently, President Joe Biden pushed through Congress a $1.1 trillion bill to begin to remedy these infrastructure problems.

(Source: https://www.cfr.org/backgrounder/state-us-infrastructure)

## #14 International Terrorism

The jihadist terrorist threat to the United States is relatively limited. Since the 9/11 attacks, no foreign terrorist organization has successfully directed and carried out a deadly attack inside the United States. With ISIS' territorial collapse, the threat posed by the group has receded. It has been more than a year since the last deadly jihadist terrorist attack, and the number of terrorism-related cases in the United States has declined substantially since its peak in 2015, though there will almost certainly be an uptick in cases this year.

When it comes to the jihadist terrorist threat, the main threat remains terrorists inspired by ISIS as opposed to ISIS-directed attacks of the sort seen in Paris in 2015 and Brussels in 2016. The most typical jihadist threat to the United States remains homegrown rather than from foreign nationals infiltrating the country. The travel ban is not an effective response to this threat.

**Cost**: (Amount of money estimated to fix the problem) Of the $2.8 trillion in U.S. CT spending, homeland security spending totaled $979 billion or 35 percent, emergency and OCO spending at DOD totaled $1.7 trillion or 60 percent, war-related spending at State/USAID totaled $138 billion or 5 percent. Non-CT foreign aid totaled $11 billion.

(Source: https://www.stimson.org/wp- content/files/file attachm ents/CT_Spending_Report_0.pd

# #15 Sexism

Recent social research conducted has found the enjoyment of sexist humor to be strongly correlated with sexual aggression towards women among male college students. In addition, studies have shown that exposure to sexist humor, particularly humor related to sexual assault, can increase male aggression and their tendency to discriminate against women. One study also asserted that the attitude behind such humor creates an environment where such discriminatory and possibly violent behavior is acceptable. Men's tendency to self-report the likelihood that they would commit sexually violent acts has also been found to increase after exposure to sexist humor, as reported by researchers.

Research from Lawrence University has found that men were more likely to be hired in traditionally masculine jobs, such as sales management, and women were more likely to be hired in traditionally feminine jobs, such as receptionist or secretary. However, individuals of either gender with masculine personality traits were advantaged when applying for either masculine or feminine jobs, indicating a possibly valuing of stereotypically male traits above stereotypically female traits.

The inequality faced by women, inequality, prejudsice, and violence against transgender men and women, as well as gender nonconforming individuals and non-binary individuals, are also prevalent in the United States. There are real dollar costs in failing to address these problems because individuals suffer from prejudices in the workforce and employment, higher levels of domestic violence, higher rates of hate crimes, especially murder, and higher levels of police brutality when compared to the cisgender population.

**Cost:** (Amount of money estimated to fix the problem) Women's and girls' economic security will likely receive $2 billion for educational programs. At the Summit for Democracy in December, the United States also announced the new $3.35 billion initiative for advancing women's and girls' civic and political leadership.

(Source : https://carnegieendowment.org/2022/03/22/how-u.s.-gender-equality-funding-increase-can-actually-be-effective-pub-86686)

## Conclusions

The United States has been at war and belligerent for 200 years since its founding. In the first hundred years of America's existence, these wars were won, laying the foundation for the United States to be the fourth-largest country in the world in terms of land area. It can be said that the United States benefited from these wars, forming the American character of “a stick in one hand and a carrot in the other.” At the same time, many people in the United States hold a gun. We have seen too many shootings in our daily lives. In international affairs, we have seen too many wars with American involvement. Why can't we treat each other as equals and negotiate amicably in all matters? Why do we have to solve problems by force at every turn? Is there an element of militarism in the cultural DNA of the United States?

In World War II, the United States led the world war against fascism as the righteous side and won the war. In that era, the United States played the role of a good world policeman. It was America’s duty and responsibility that deserve recognition and win the trust and respect of the world. After World War II, the United States became the global hegemon and began to rule the world according to its own will. Looking back at these 78 years of history after the end of World War II, we must ask whether the performance of the United States as the world’s policeman in these 78 years is good enough. Has the United States, as the world’s policeman, abused its power, killed innocent people indiscriminately, and committed bad acts of corruption and embezzlement? Did the United States, as the world’s policeman, bring peace to the local people in those wars after World War II, or did it bring one powder keg after another?

America is the most powerful country in the world, but is the American model of society the most perfect and only model in the world? Can the United States shoot at will if it does not follow the will of the United States and does not submit to the interests of the United States?

Mankind has thousands of years of civilization, and mankind has enough wisdom to keep improving our civilization. America has now accumulated heaps of domestic problems; America's own social model, America's own civilization, and values need to be rethought and improved. It is very dangerous to be a police officer without a proper concept of law enforcement. The United States does not have to go to the world with a gun to enforce the law and fight a war before its own problems are solved. The United States has always been the most important country in the world in terms of human rights. But the irony is that the United States does not really respect every human life, every human right. Nor does it treat countries other than the United States equally. If the United States had done so, Floyd would be on earth instead of in heaven at this moment. Iraq and Afghanistan, too, would not be a mess.

The United States has been the world's policeman for 78 years. Frankly, it's tiring, and it is time to take a break. The world, as it is, is wonderful. The world's civilization and economy are already very developed and prosperous. So, we don't need so many policemen anymore, we just need more builders.

Humanity has an ugly side, though, and violence is an unchangeable internal cause. However, we still have to believe that humans have strong egos. In the next hundred years, the wise Americans will be wise enough to stop shooting at random. Through peaceful means, we will solve our own problems and create a more prosperous civilization. For this world, bring more excitement.

## Bibliography

"Americans' Views of the Problems Facing the Nation." Pew Research Center - U.S. Politics & Policy. Pew Research Center, July 25, 2022. https://www.pewresearch.org/politics/2021/04/15/americans-views-of-the-problems-facing-the-nation/.

"Costs of Major Us Wars." Naval History and Heritage Command. https://www.history.navy.mil/research/library/online-reading-room/title-list-alphabetically/c/costs-major-us-wars.html.

"Defense Spending by Country 2022." https://worldpopulationreview.com/country-rankings/defense-spending-by-country.

"Peace, But at What Cost?" Encyclopedia.com. https://www.encyclopedia.com/history/educational-magazines/peace-what-cost.

# Chapter 5

# Is America Corrupt?

## What is Corruption?

*The Oxford Dictionary* defines corruption as dishonest or fraudulent conduct by those in power, typically involving bribery. Similar words: unscrupulousness, deceit, deception, duplicity, double-dealing. Corruption is a form of dishonesty or a criminal offense undertaken by a person or an organization entrusted in a position of authority to acquire illicit benefits or abuse power for personal gain. The most common types or categories of corruption are supply versus demand, grand versus petty, conventional versus unconventional, and public versus private corruption.

## Causes of Public Sector Corruption

A variety of factors at the country level have an impact on how governments and their services function, which in turn influences the existence and prevalence of public sector corruption that includes the government, corporations, and individuals. To what degree does America is corrupt based on the following causes?

## Country Size

Research shows that geographically large countries with a low population density can be more prone to corruption because of the increased difficulties in monitoring public officials in dispersed locations (Goel and Nelson, 2010).

According to the World Population Review, America ranks 161 in the population density list with 36 persons/km compared with the number one most densely populated country in the world, Monaco, with 19,361/persons km. Russia ranks 199 with a density of 9/persons km. According to this theory, Monaco should be the least corrupt country in the world. Iceland, with a density of 4/persons km, ranking 209, should be the most corrupt out of the list of recognized countries.

Here is the list of countries per population density in the range of 5 above and five below America. Does this prove the corruption by country size theorem?

| | | | | |
|---|---|---|---|---|
| 155 | DR Congo | 41 | 99,010,212 | 2,344,858 km² |
| 156 | Mozambique | 41 | 32,969,518 | 801,590 km² |
| 157 | Turks and Caicos Islands | 41 | 45,703 | 948 km² |
| 158 | Bahamas | 40 | 409,984 | 13,943 km² |
| 159 | Palau | 40 | 18,055 | 459 km² |
| 160 | Zimbabwe | 39 | 16,320,537 | 390,757 km² |

| 161 | United States | 36 | 338,289,857 | 9,372,610 km² |
|---|---|---|---|---|
| 162 | Eritrea | 36 | 3,684,032 | 117,600 km² |
| 163 | Kyrgyzstan | 35 | 6,630,623 | 199,951 km² |
| 164 | Faroe Islands | 35 | 53,090 | 1,393 km² |
| 165 | Venezuela | 33 | 28,301,696 | 916,445 km² |

**Country Age**

Newly independent countries, or those that have recently transitioned from authoritarian regimes to democracies, may face more corruption owing to, for example, underdeveloped governance systems or unregulated opportunities created by the privatization of state assets (Goel and Nelson, 2010). In the context of corruption, unregulated opportunities mean increasing one's share of existing wealth using public resources without creating new wealth for the state.

According to Oldest.org, the oldest countries in the world and the years they were founded can be compared below.

Egypt c. 6000 BCE
India c. 3300 BCE
Afghanistan, c. 3000 BCE
China, c. 2070 BCE
Georgia, c. 1500 BCE
Ethiopia, 980 BCE
Greece, c. 800 BCE
Japan, c. 660 BCE

Iran, c. 550 BCE
San Marino, c. 301 CE

According to this theorem, since the United States was founded only in 1789 CE, therefore, it is one of the youngest nations in the world at only 233 years old, and that proves it is one of the most corrupt countries.

**Natural Resources**

The public sector monopoly over the distribution and allocation of natural resources rights allows economic opportunities to be exploited for corrupt purposes. The website of the Natural Resource Governance Institute stresses that "given their highly concentrated and highly profitable nature, the oil, gas and mining industries can generate the kind of political and private incentives that favor unregulated opportunities and institutional (or state) capture." Indeed, data show that many resource-rich countries suffer from poor governance and systemic corruption (Natural Resource Governance Institute, 2019).

According to Invetopidea.com, Natural resources are commodities, the raw inputs used to make everything we use, from intermediate goods to finished products. These resources are found in the earth among reserves yet to be extracted.

Renewable resources are those with supply not diminished by use, including solar power, wind power, and hydroelectric energy. Nonrenewable resources like fossil fuels and mined metals have finite reserves depleted by extraction. Natural resources are found throughout the world, though the deposits tend to clump as a result of geological processes.

According to Invetopidea.com, the 10 countries with the greatest natural resources are:

1. Russia
2. United States
3. Saudi Arabia
4. Canada
5. Iran
6. China
7. Brazil
8. Australia
9. Iraq
10. Venezuela

Can we then say, according to the above theorem of corruption by natural resources, that these are the 10 most corrupt countries in the world?

**Political Instability**

Political stability is associated with low corruption levels, whereas the probability of corruption is higher in politically unstable environments (Lederman, Loayza, and Soares, 2005). Lack of stability in transitions to a newly elected government is particularly associated with public sector corruption. Notably, partisan administration can be the cause of corruption in certain countries.

According to the worldpopulationreview.com's 2022 Fragile States Index, the 10 most politically unstable countries in the world, from 162 countries ranked, are:

1. South Sudan
2. Somalia
3. Yemen
4. Syria
5. Central African Republic
6. Democratic Republic of Congo
7. Sudan
8. Chad
9. Afghanistan
10. Zimbabwe

The United States is ranked 142 on the list of 162 countries instability. Therefore, can we conclude that America is corrupt based on the theorem that the more stable a country is, the less corruption exists in that country?

**Wages**

Low wages and the resulting poverty in the public sector are also believed to contribute to corruption in some countries (Tanzi, 1998). Countries by wages, according to worldpopulationreview.com:

10 Countries with the Highest Median Income, 2021 (in US Dollars/annual):
Luxembourg - 26,321.
United Arab Emirates - 24,292.

Norway - 22,684.
Switzerland - 21,490.
United States - 19,306.
Canada - 18,652.
Austria - 18,405.
Sweden - 17,625.

10 Countries with the Lowest Median Income, 2021 (in US Dollars/annual):
Rwanda – 621.
Uzbekistan – 591.
Zambia – 545.
Mozambique - 529.
Central African Republic – 491.
Guinea Bissau – 486
Malawi – 484.
Madagascar – 398.
DR Congo – 395.
Angola - 365.

According to the theorem that low wages and the resulting poverty in the public sector are believed to contribute to corruption, can we say that America is corrupt?

As we move through the following theorems on the various causes of corruption in the countries on earth, we will see a continued pattern of the countries where there are the following causes of corruption, and we will notice generally the same results as have been shown above. Generally, it can be stated that countries with the resources to take care of their population through natural and economic sources, with adherence to fair and just laws, with a robust system of social services support for their people, with a vision of growth and prosperity—these countries will be less prone to corruption. Without going through detailed research on each of the below causes of corruption through country-by-country comparisons, as we have done above, we can start to come to some general conclusions about corruption in America and wealthier countries. In subsequent sections of this chapter, we will examine the subject in more detailed ways to expose the corruption that certainly does exist in America.

## Additional Causes for Corruption

### Lack of Rule of Law

Lawlessness or the poor rule of law is an important government-level contributor to corruption. The probability of corruption occurring might increase when the legal system cannot provide sanctions for officials that engage in corruption (La Porta and others, 1999; Treisman, 2000). In addition, corruption risks are higher in countries with less secure property rights, as corrupt means are used to ensure the security of these rights, where the legal system cannot do so (Dong and Tongler, 2011).

### Failure of Governance

Shah (E4J University Module Series on Anti-Corruption, 2006) states that public sector corruption results from a failure of governance. Poor governance can arise from low-quality public sector management, a lack of accountability, poor relations between the government and citizens, a weak legal framework, a lack of transparency regarding public sector processes, and poor dissemination of information. A lack of competence and capacity due to inadequate training also contributes to the failure of governance. The link between good governance and anti-corruption is critical to understand.

### Size of Government

The research presents mixed findings on the relationship between corruption and the size of government. According to Goel and Nelson (2010) and Rose-Ackerman and Palifka (2016), the larger the government, the more numerous the opportunities for unregulated opportunities by officials. In contrast, Gerring and Thacker (2005) find that the size of the government is not correlated to higher levels of corruption. One conclusion that can be drawn from the mixed research findings is that the relationship between corruption and the size of government depends on other factors such as regime type, political stability, and government structure, or federal versus centralized systems.

### Nature of Bureaucracy

Tanzi (1998), Kaufman and Wei (1999), and Goel and Nelson (2010) all contend that government bureaucracy and government intervention in the economy promotes corruption. Tanzi (1998) further asserts that “the existence of regulations and authorizations gives a kind of monopoly power to the officials who must authorize or inspect the activity." He also specifies the quality of the bureaucracy as an important causative factor for corruption.

## Public Spending at the Local Level

A study by Corrado and Rossetti (2018) addresses public corruption in various local regions. Their findings suggest that "regions which have historically placed less importance on rooting out corruption may be stuck in a vicious circle of higher levels of corruption" and that "individuals who reside in regions where corruption is higher and persistent are less likely to be satisfied with public services."

## Social Capital

Social capital refers to the "links, shared values and understandings in society that enable individuals and groups to trust each other and so work together" (OECD, 2007c, p. 102). The study of Corrado and Rossetti (2018) found that regions with higher social capital are more likely to face lower levels of corruption. Their results confirm the studies that higher levels of social capital are associated with less corruption. However, it is unclear whether social capital leads to less corruption or whether low corruption leads to greater social capital.

## Large Unique Projects

Locatelli and others (2017) analyze different types of corruption and projects that are corruption prone. Their findings suggest that when public actors play a key role in "large unique projects" - i.e., publicly funded projects which occur once and have no predecessor to provide guidance - these projects are more likely to be affected by corruption compared to smaller and more routine projects.

## Conflicts of Interest

Conflict of interest has been defined by the Organization for Economic Cooperation and Development (OECD, 2003) as "a conflict between the public duty and private interest of public officials, in which public officials have private-capacity interests which could improperly influence the performance of their official duties and responsibilities." An example of a conflict of interest includes the "revolving door" situation, in which public officials obtain lucrative posts in the private sector once they leave the public service, with the expectation that they will use their public sector contacts to benefit the private company (Ferguson, 2017). The types of "private interests" that could lead to a conflict of interest include objectives like a directorship in a company but can also include subjective ideological, political, and personal interests that may improperly influence public duties (Ferguson, 2017; Rose-Ackerman, 2014). The existence of a conflict of interest in and of itself is not necessarily unlawful. What is unlawful, however, is the failure to disclose a conflict of interest and/or the mishandling of it.

## Transparency International

### What is Transparency International ("TI")?

According to TI's own website (www.transparency.org), TI states:

"TI and its Corruption Perceptions Index (CPI) "is the most widely used global corruption ranking in the world. It measures how corrupt each country's public sector is perceived to be, according to experts and businesspeople. Transparency International is a global movement working in over 100 countries to end the injustice of corruption.

We focus on issues with the greatest impact on people's lives and hold the powerful to account for the common good. Through our advocacy, campaigning, and research, we work to expose the systems and networks that enable corruption to thrive, demanding greater transparency and integrity in all areas of public life. Our mission is to stop corruption and promote transparency, accountability, and integrity at all levels and across all sectors of society. Our vision is a world in which government, politics, business, civil society, and the daily lives of people are free of corruption. We are independent, non-governmental, not-for-profit, and we work with like-minded partners worldwide to end the injustice of corruption."

[65] Transparency International (TI) is a nonpartisan, nonprofit, nongovernmental organization (NGO) founded in Berlin in 1993 to expose corruption and reduce its harmful effects worldwide, especially on the poor and underprivileged. TI consists of a global network of approximately 100 national chapters devoted to fighting corruption in their home countries. The headquarters are in Berlin.

TI does not conduct investigations into corruption itself but instead brings together officials in the areas of government, business, civil society, and the media to promote transparency in private and public

---

[65] Britannica, T. Editors of Encyclopaedia, "Transparency International," Encyclopedia Britannica, February 23, 2011, https://www.britannica.com/topic/Transparency-International.

affairs and to lobby for anticorruption measures. TI targets corruption at every level, from local governments to multinational corporations, in keeping with its belief that corruption creates and perpetuates poverty, weakens democracy, distorts national and international trade, endangers national security, and threatens natural resources around the world. It focuses on five areas of concern: corruption in politics, corruption in the private sector, corruption in public contracting, poverty and development, and international anticorruption conventions.

TI is governed by a board of directors, which is elected at an annual meeting of national chapters and individual members. It publishes several annual reports, including the *Global Corruption Report*, the *Global Corruption Barometer*, and the *Corruption Perceptions Index*, which ranks countries by perceived level of corruption based on surveys of experts. It also publishes books on specific regions and issues Integrity Awards to individuals who expose corruption in their countries.

## Allegations of the Institutional Hypocrisy of Transparency International

### A) Bully and Sexual Harassment.

In 2016, the International Secretariat of Transparency International (TI-S), arguably the world's most influential anti-corruption NGO, was embarking on a so-call fundamental "reform" process in response to a series of bullying and sexual harassment scandals in the office. In the end, thirty-six former senior staff members fell victim to this reform. They were dismissed by the then Managing Director (MD), Mr. Cobus de Swardt, who was the legal implementer and an important accomplice of this muddy reform. However, two months later, Mr. de Swardt was also thrown out as the Managing Director in the same crude manner and was replaced by the then Vice Chair of the International Board of Directors of Transparency International, who coveted this well-paid job for many years. It was precisely for this purpose that she and the Chair proposed various schemes to "reform" the International Secretariat of TI. In the end, she achieved it!

By then, Mr. de Swardt totally forgot about how badly he had previously mistreated his staff in the TI-S but felt that he was unfairly humbled and cheated. For many years under his management, TI-S had been accused of promoting a "toxic" internal office culture of bullying and harassment. Only when he himself suffered did he undertake to change suddenly into a victim. Mr. de Swardt wrote numerous whistleblower complaints to international donor agencies which funded TI and carefully chronicled "the ethical breakdown over a 5-year period starting in 2015" in TI-S while shamelessly cutting himself out from the decadent office culture. He got himself up as a whistleblower and charged that "TI-S has become trapped in a vicious cycle of secrecy, corruption, and lies."

**B) Funding.**

As a result, funding from various international donor agencies to TI-S has greatly shrunken. The team for the International Anti-Corruption Conference (IACC) announced in April 2022 that the 20th IACC would be held online. But just some days later, that changed, and it was announced that the 20th IACC of 2022 would be convened in Washington D.C. on 6 December 2022 and hosted by the United States government. Obviously, TI-S, a once reputable NGO which had long boasted of its professionalism and independence for a long time, has abandoned these policies and kneeled down before the Biden Administration. TI-S even shifts from its previous position of "Corruption takes place in every country with a different political system" to "uprooting corruption and defending democratic values."

The IACC is an international forum for bringing together heads of state, civil society, the private sector, and others to tackle the challenges of corruption. The IACC was established in 1983 and usually convenes every two years in different regions worldwide. However, due to a lack of resources, it was reduced to a commercial event, competed by whatever governments needed it desperately as a whitewashing political show. Whoever can pay the US $6 million dollars to TI-S can host an IACC in its own country. Consequently, it was often involved with political controversies. Below are just a few examples:

**C) The Panama Papers**.

In 2016, an anonymous whistleblower "John Doe" leaked 11.5 million leaked documents (or 2.6 terabytes of data) to a German journalist Bastian Obermayer from the newspaper *Süd- Deutsche Zeitung* (SZ). The documents were created by and taken from a former Panamanian offshore law firm and corporate service provider Mossack Fonseca. The papers detail financial and attorney-client information for more than 214,488 offshore entities' personal financial information about wealthy individuals and public officials that had previously been kept private in Panama. Hence it was called the Panama Papers and was published on April 3, 2016. The International Consortium of Investigative Journalists (ICIJ) posted the full document on its website. As a response, the then-president of Panama, Juan Carlos Varela, announced the creation of a new judiciary tribunal and a high-level commission led by Nobel Prize Laureate Joseph Stiglitz to investigate the case.

As the scandal was simmering and sweeping through the country, TI-S ran the IACC in Panama City again! It is simple logic to understand who would need such an anti-corruption conference and who would benefit from it. Ironically, it was in Panama, during the Annual Membership Meeting of TI-S that the trade council of TI-S went into a severe debate with the senior management of TI-S and questioned its financial recourses and integrity!

**D) The 1MDB Scandal.**

In 2015, a major political scandal-hit Malaysian government: a document leak showed that Malaysia's then-Prime Minister Najib Razak had channeled over RM 2.67 billion (US $700 million) into his personal bank accounts from 1 Malaysia Development Berhad (1MDB), a government-run strategic development company. The revelations triggered protests and backlash in Malaysia. To bail out himself out of this political scandal, Najib Razak paid US $6 million to TI-S and received the bid to host the IACC in Kuala Lumpur. Whilst the IACC was going on in Kuala Lumpur, the city was filled with angry protesters against Najib Razak. But it didn't stop the Chair of TI-S from talking loudly and spluttering with pride about “fighting against corruption” in the IACC. He conspired with the vice chair to grab the managing director position and rewarded them the vice chair. In the outside world, people always learn about the explicit commitment to protecting whistleblowers proclaimed by TI-S and receive its often-repeated press releases and statements in favor of an EU Directive that would oblige member governments to protect whistleblowers, whereas, inside TI, the senior management has no shame in committing such internal misconduct. This is institutional hypocrisy.

**D) The Red-Shirt Protests in Bangkok.**

In 2010, Thailand experienced a series of coups. Since the government took office a year ago, four ministers have resigned, three over corruption scandals, citing graft-busting as one of its priorities.

From March to May 2010, Thailand endured the most violent confrontations since the protests against military rule in 1992. At least 90 people died, and more than 2,000 were wounded in clashes between security forces and anti-government protesters led by the United Front for Democracy against Dictatorship (UDD), also known as “Red Shirts.” Arson attacks in Bangkok and elsewhere caused billions of dollars of damage.

Contentious key issues, such as high-level corruption, the role of the monarchy and military in Thai politics and society, a dysfunctional and corrupt political system, the failure to hold powerful individuals across the political spectrum accountable for human rights abuses, widespread economic disparities, and a deep rural-urban divide were key catalysts for the protests.

| Score | Country | Rank |
|---|---|---|
| 88 | Denmark | 1 |
| 88 | Finland | 1 |
| 88 | New Zealand | 1 |
| 85 | Norway | 4 |
| 85 | Singapore | 4 |
| 85 | Sweden | 4 |
| 84 | Switzerland | 7 |
| 82 | Netherlands | 8 |
| 81 | Luxembourg | 9 |
| 80 | Germany | 10 |
| 78 | United Kingdom | 11 |
| 74 | Austria | 13 |
| 74 | Canada | 13 |
| 74 | Estonia | 13 |
| 74 | Ireland | 13 |
| 62 | Portugal | 32 |
| 61 | Spain | 34 |
| 61 | Lithuania | 34 |
| 59 | Israel | 36 |
| 59 | Latvia | 36 |

| Score | Country | Rank |
|---|---|---|
| 74 | Iceland | 13 |
| 73 | Australia | 18 |
| 73 | Belgium | 18 |
| 73 | Japan | 18 |
| 73 | Uruguay | 18 |
| 71 | France | 22 |
| 70 | Seychelles | 23 |
| 69 | United Arab Emirates | 24 |
| 68 | Bhutan | 25 |
| 67 | Chile | 27 |
| 67 | United States of America | 27 |
| 65 | Barbados | 29 |
| 64 | Bahamas | 30 |
| 63 | Qatar | 31 |
| 62 | Korea, South | 32 |
| 45 | Romania | 66 |
| 45 | Tome and Principe Sao | 66 |
| 45 | Vanuatu | 66 |
| 44 | Jamaica | 70 |
| 44 | Tunisia | 70 |

| Score | Country | Rank |
|---|---|---|
| 59 | Saint Vincent and the Grenadines | 36 |
| 58 | Cabo Verde | 39 |
| 58 | Costa Rica | 39 |
| 57 | Slovenia | 41 |
| 56 | Italy | 42 |
| 56 | Saint Lucia | 42 |
| 56 | Poland | 42 |
| 55 | Botswana | 45 |
| 55 | Dominica | 45 |
| 55 | Fiji | 45 |
| 55 | Georgia | 45 |
| 54 | Czech Republic | 49 |
| 54 | Malta | 49 |
| 54 | Mauritius | 49 |
| 53 | Cyprus | 52 |
| 53 | Grenada | 52 |
| 53 | Rwanda | 52 |
| 53 | Saudi Arabia | 52 |
| 52 | Oman | 56 |
| 52 | Slovakia | 56 |

| Score | Country | Rank |
|---|---|---|
| 44 | South Africa | 70 |
| 43 | Ghana | 73 |
| 43 | Hungary | 73 |
| 43 | Kuwait | 73 |
| 43 | Senegal | 73 |
| 43 | Solomon Islands | 73 |
| 42 | Benin | 78 |
| 42 | Burkina Faso | 78 |
| 42 | Bulgaria | 78 |
| 42 | Bahrain | 78 |
| 41 | Belarus | 82 |
| 41 | Timor-Leste | 82 |
| 41 | Trinidad and Tobago | 82 |
| 40 | India | 85 |
| 40 | Maldives | 85 |
| 39 | Colombia | 87 |
| 39 | Ethiopia | 87 |
| 39 | Guyana | 87 |
| 39 | Kosovo | 87 |
| 39 | Morocco | 87 |

| Score | Country | Rank |
|---|---|---|
| 49 | Armenia | 58 |
| 49 | Greece | 58 |
| 49 | Jordan | 58 |
| 49 | Namibia | 58 |
| 48 | Malaysia | 62 |
| 47 | Croatia | 63 |
| 46 | Cuba | 64 |
| 46 | Montenegro | 64 |
| 38 | Lesotho | 96 |
| 38 | Serbia | 96 |
| 38 | Turkey | 96 |
| 37 | Gambia | 102 |
| 37 | Kazakhstan | 102 |
| 37 | Sri Lanka | 102 |
| 36 | Cote d'Ivoire | 105 |
| 36 | Ecuador | 105 |
| 36 | Moldova | 105 |
| 36 | Panama | 105 |
| 36 | Peru | 105 |
| 35 | Albania | 110 |
| 35 | Bosnia and Herzegovina | 110 |
| 35 | Mongolia | 110 |
| 35 | Malawi | 110 |
| 35 | Thailand | 110 |

| Score | Country | Rank |
|---|---|---|
| 39 | North Macedonia | 87 |
| 39 | Suriname | 87 |
| 39 | Tanzania | 87 |
| 39 | Vietnam | 87 |
| 38 | Argentina | 96 |
| 38 | Brazil | 96 |
| 38 | Indonesia | 96 |
| 30 | Laos | 128 |
| 30 | Paraguay | 128 |
| 30 | Togo | 128 |
| 29 | Angola | 136 |
| 29 | Liberia | 136 |
| 29 | Mali | 136 |
| 29 | Russia | 136 |
| 28 | Myanmar | 140 |
| 28 | Mauritania | 140 |
| 28 | Pakistan | 140 |
| 28 | Uzbekistan | 140 |
| 27 | Cameroon | 144 |
| 27 | Kyrgyzstan | 144 |
| 27 | Uganda | 144 |
| 26 | Bangladesh | 147 |
| 26 | Madagascar | 147 |
| 26 | Mozambique | 147 |

| Score | Country | Rank |
|---|---|---|
| 34 | Sierra Leone | 115 |
| 34 | El Salvador | 115 |
| 33 | Algeria | 117 |
| 33 | Egypt | 117 |
| 33 | Nepal | 117 |
| 33 | Philippines | 117 |
| 33 | Zambia | 117 |
| 32 | Eswatini | 122 |
| 32 | Ukraine | 122 |
| 31 | Gabon | 124 |
| 31 | Mexico | 124 |
| 31 | Niger | 124 |
| 31 | Papua New Guinea | 124 |
| 30 | Azerbaijan | 128 |
| 30 | Bolivia | 128 |
| 30 | Djibouti | 128 |
| 30 | Dominican Republic | 128 |
| 30 | Kenya | 128 |
| 20 | Sudan | 164 |
| 20 | Chad | 164 |
| 19 | Burundi | 169 |

| Score | Country | Rank |
|---|---|---|
| 25 | Guinea | 150 |
| 25 | Guatemala | 150 |
| 25 | Iran | 150 |
| 25 | Tajikistan | 150 |
| 24 | Central African Republic | 154 |
| 24 | Lebanon | 154 |
| 24 | Nigeria | 154 |
| 23 | Honduras | 157 |
| 23 | Iraq | 157 |
| 23 | Cambodia | 157 |
| 23 | Zimbabwe | 157 |
| 22 | Eritrea | 161 |
| 21 | Congo | 162 |
| 21 | Guinea Bissau | 162 |
| 20 | Comoros | 164 |
| 20 | Haiti | 164 |
| 20 | Nicaragua | 164 |
| 16 | Afghanistan | 174 |
| 16 | North Korea | 174 |
| 16 | Yemen | 174 |
| 14 | Venezuela | 177 |

| Score | Country | Rank |
|---|---|---|
| 19 | Democratic Republic of the Congo | 169 |
| 19 | Turkmenistan | 169 |
| 17 | Equatorial Guinea | 172 |
| 17 | Libya | 172 |

| Score | Country | Rank |
|---|---|---|
| 13 | Somalia | 178 |
| 13 | Syria | 178 |
| 11 | South Sudan | 180 |
| | | |

**Documented Controversies by Transparency International**

**A) Failure to Weigh Corruption by Each Country**

According to the newspaper *Le Monde*: "In its main surveys, Transparency International does not measure the weight of corruption in economic terms for each country. It develops a Corruption Perception Index (CPI) based on surveys conducted by private structures or other NGOs: the Economist Intelligence Unit, backed by the British liberal weekly newspaper *The Economist*, the American neoconservative organization Freedom House, the World Economic Forum, or large corporations. The IPC ignores corruption cases that concern the business world. So, the collapse of Lehman Brothers (2008) or the manipulation of the money market reference rate (Libor) by major British banks revealed in 2011 did not affect the ratings of the United States or the United Kingdom." The organization also receives funding from companies that are themselves convicted of corruption offences. CPI's reliance on the opinions of a relatively small group of experts and businesspeople has been criticized by some. Alex Cobham, the fellow at the Center for Global Development, states that it "embeds a powerful and misleading elite bias in popular perceptions of corruption." Others argue it is not plausible ever to measure the true scale and depth of a highly complex issue like corruption with a single number and then rank countries accordingly[66].

**B) 2013 Non-Support of Edward Snowden**

At its annual members' meeting in November 2013 in Berlin, Transparency International's national chapters from Germany and Ireland proposed a resolution calling for the " To end of the prosecution of Edward J. Snowden. He should be recognized as a whistleblower for his help to reveal the over-reaching and unlawful surveillance by secret services. He symbolizes the courage of numerous other whistleblowers around the world."

The final resolution that was passed by the plenary excluded any reference to Snowden and excluded a call for "comprehensive protection on whistleblowers from all forms of retaliation." The original resolution was weakened following the intervention of the USA chapter. Five months earlier, in June 2013, representatives from Transparency International declined Snowden's request to meet him at the Moscow airport. Amnesty International and Human

---

[66] "Is Transparency International's Measure of Corruption Still Valid?" *The Guardian*, December 3, 2013, https://www.theguardian.com/global-development/poverty-matters/2013/dec/03/transparency-international-measure-corruption-valid.

Rights Watch met Snowden to support his asylum request, but Transparency International refused[67].

## C) 2014 Funding from Siemens

In January 2015, it was reported that Transparency International accepted $3 million from the German engineering multinational Siemens, which in 2008 paid one of the largest corporate corruption fines in history – $1.6 billion – for bribing government officials in numerous countries. In 2014, Siemens made the donation to Transparency International after pleading guilty in 2008 to bribery charges relating to widespread corrupt practices in Greece, Norway, Iraq, Vietnam, Italy, Israel, Argentina, Venezuela, and Russia.

Transparency International applied for and received the funding from Siemens, even though TI's due diligence procedures prohibit the organization from accepting money from corporations that want to "greenwash" their reputations by making donations to TI. "If any corporate donor is accused of having been involved in corruption, the donor can expect no protection from TI," the procedures state. Transparency International received the funding from the *Siemens Integrity Initiative* about a year after the *Initiative* hired former TI staffer Jana Mittermaier, raising questions of a "revolving door" that has benefited both the organization and the company.

---

67 "Whistleblower Protection of Edward Snowden," TI-Germany and TI- Ireland, February 10, 2014.

Several of TI's national chapters also have accepted money from Siemens: $660,000 for TI USA, $600,000 for TI Italy, $450,000 for TI Bulgaria, and $230,000 for TI Mexico – each for a period of three years. "This really shows that Transparency International is not as pure as people think," a TI insider told *Corporate Crime Reporter*. Transparency International Managing Director at the time, *Cobus de Swardt*, said, "We did not file an application to Siemens, we applied to the Siemens Integrity Initiative. There's a difference. We have not applied to Siemens." However, according to Siemens, the money for these grants is "provided by Siemens."[68]

**D) 2015 Whistleblowing**

In August 2015 former TI staffer Anna Buzzoni went public regarding retaliation she and her colleagues faced after reporting to managers questionable financial dealings at TI's Water Integrity Network. Two of Buzzoni's project responsibilities were suspended, and she was transferred against her will. She left TI shortly before internal whistleblower guidelines were adopted in June 2014[69].

**E) 2015 Croatia Chapter Disaccreditation**

Due to a "lack of confidence," TI's chapter in Croatia was disaccredited by the organization's board of directors in November 2015. The previous year, several leaders of the Croatia chapter

---

[68] "Integrity Initiative," http://www.siemens.com/.

[69] Frederik Richter, "Falling on Deaf Ears," correctiv.org, August 27, 2015, https://correctiv.org/en/latest-stories/corruption/2015/08/27/falling-on-deaf-ears/.

challenged the legality of the chapter president's election. The president was accused of falsifying records, having conflicts of interest, and arbitrarily expelling 10 chapter members who opposed staff hiring against the organization's rules. The Croatian government eventually revoked the president's appointment[70].

### F) 2017 USA Chapter Disaccreditation

In January 2017, the TI Secretariat confirmed that its International Board of Directors decided on 10 January 2017 to strip its US affiliate – Transparency International USA – of its accreditation as the National Chapter in the United States. The stated basis for the disaccreditation was the board's recognition of differences in philosophies, strategies, and priorities between the former chapter and the Transparency International Movement. Elsewhere, it was reported that TI-USA came to be seen in the United States as a corporate front group funded by multinational corporations. TI-USA's funding was provided by Bechtel Corporation, Deloitte, Google, Pfizer ($50,000 or more), Citigroup, ExxonMobil, Fluor, General Electric, Lockheed Martin, Marsh & McLennan, PepsiCo, PricewaterhouseCoopers, Raytheon, Realogy, Tyco ($25,000–$49,999), and Freeport-McMoRan and Johnson & Johnson (up to $24,999). TI-USA previously awarded an annual corporate leadership award to one of its big corporate funders. In 2016, this award went to Bechtel. In April 2015,

---

70 "Transparency International Statement on Its Former Chapter in Croatia...," Transparency.org, https://www.transparency.org/en/press/transparency-international-statement-on-its-former-chapter-in-croatia.

the Secretariat defended the decision by TI-USA to give Hillary Clinton its Integrity Award in 2012. Since January 1, 2020, Transparency International has had an office in the United States[71].

**G) 2017–21 Reports of Bullying, Harassment, and Abuse of Power by TI Board Members and Senior Management.**

In 2017, Cobus de Swardt stood down as Transparency International's Managing Director following a dispute with the organization's Board of Directors. De Swardt agreed on a settlement with Transparency International in a Labor Court in Berlin.

In August 2019, accounts from seven current and former TI Secretariat staff were reported in *The Guardian* alleging a "toxic" workplace culture at the organization.

De Swardt's successor, Patricia Moreira, left in 2020 after making similar accusations to those of De Swardt, accusing the Board of failing to protect whistleblowers, as well as corruption.

The German newspaper *Frankfurter Allgemeine Zeitung* reported that Transparency International dismissed Moreira "without giving any reasons." The article added that "dozens of employees, including high-ranking ones, have left the organization in recent

---

[71] Editor, "Transparency International Strips United States Affiliate of Accreditation," *Corporate Crime Reporter*, January 19, 2017, https://www.corporatecrimereporter.com/news/200/transparency-international-strips-us-affiliate-of-accreditation/.

years. Even long-standing and deeply committed employees complain that TI is involved in political intrigues in which some are only interested in their own progress. For a non-governmental organization whose goal is to fight corruption around the world and which collects millions of dollars in funding from governments and companies every year, this is a disturbing finding."

In 2021, de Swardt published a book accusing Transparency International of abuse of power and silencing whistleblowers. De Swardt also presented a video published on YouTube by his publisher, Springer, criticizing corruption at Transparency International.

Daniel Eriksson was appointed Interim Managing Director in March 2020[72].

**H) Political Activities in Brazil**

Transparency International's political impartiality, as well as its own transparency, have been called into question over hacked conversations of prosecutors in Operation Car Wash, leaked to *The Intercept*. In these, chief prosecutor Deltan Dallagnol and head of TI Brazil, Bruno Brandão, discuss a "backstage campaign" to "disarm resistance on the left", fund selected candidates, and target others,

---

72 Doshi Vidhi, "Transparency International Staff Complain of Bullying and Harassment," *The Guardian*, August 21, 2019, https://www.theguardian.com/global-development/2019/aug/21/transparency-international-staff-complain-of-bullying-harassment.

seen as adversaries, using social media. Plans extended to preparing a series of false accusations ("denúncias sem materialidade") intended to damage the reputation of former president and potential candidate Luiz Inácio Lula da Silva, and lead up to a chat in which participants celebrate the election of Jair Bolsonaro.

In April 2022, Brazil's auditing court announced that it had opened an investigation against Transparency International over the illegal imprisonment of Lula da Silva[73].

### The TI Prescription is Issued, but Who Is the Patient?

The United States government has never understood what corruption is, just like it has never understood human rights. The prescription of fighting corruption stated in President Biden's National Strategy provided below is absurd and ridiculous:

- Modernizing, coordinating, and resourcing U.S. Government efforts to fight corruption:
- Curbing illicit finance and promoting beneficial ownership
- Holding Corrupt Actors Accountable:
- Preserving and strengthening the multilateral anti-corruption architecture:

---

[73] Brian Mier, "Transparency International: Brazil Court Opens Investigation of Anti-Corruption NGO," *BRASILWIRE*, April 14, 2022, https://www.brasilwire.com/brazils-auditing-court-opens-investigation-against-transparency-international/.

- Improving diplomatic engagement and leveraging foreign assistance resources to achieve anti-corruption policy goals:

The focus of these strategies is to establish a kleptocracy asset recovery rewards program that will enable the U.S. Government to kidnap, arrest and detain key foreign personnel, like Frédéric Pierucci, a former senior manager for Alstom, and Meng Wanzhou, the CFO of Huawei, in the name of anti-corruption. And then, the U.S can confiscate the assets of the relevant companies and eliminate these competitors who block the way of American company expansion. But everyone knows that they were held as "economic hostages." It had nothing to do with anti-corruption.

The Biden Administration is fully aware of the fact that nobody would be foolish enough to accept such blunt lies and political rhetoric. Therefore, it must cooperate with TI-S, using it as a fig leaf. For funding's sake, TI-S has no other choice but to lean to the United States and wave the banner of "uprooting corruption, defending democratic value." Through the IACC, the U.S. Government and TI will unite over 10,000 people from 180 countries to continue building momentum for landmark anti-corruption initiatives.

**Corruption in America**

By relying on each country's individual chapter for its annual reports instead of conducting independent research, Transparency International has been accused of not completely assessing the corruption standing of each country. Let us now examine the two major forms of corruption in America that are considered legal and illegal: Corporate Corruption and Legal Corruption.

**A) Corporate Corruption in America**

**The Military-Industrial Complex**

As previously discussed, President Dwight D. Eisenhower's farewell address to the nation on January 17, 1961, is best known for advocating that the nation guard against the potential influence of the military–industrial complex, a term he is credited with coining. This is a very important warning, so it is necessary for us to revisit it again and again.

He famously said:

> "In the councils of government, we must guard against the acquisition of unwarranted influence, whether sought or unsought, by the military-industrial complex. The potential for the disastrous rise of misplaced power exists and will persist. We must never let the weight of this combination endanger our liberties or democratic processes. We should take nothing for granted. Only an alert and knowledgeable citizenry can compel the proper meshing of the huge industrial and military machinery of defense with our peaceful methods and goals, so that security and liberty may prosper together."

The Military-Industrial Complex is a term that denotes a symbiotic relationship between a nation's military, economy, and politics.

This warning, unfortunately, has not been heeded. From recent reports, during the five-year period from 2013-2017, there were 1,059 criminal cases of defense contracting fraud resulting in the conviction of 1,087 defendants, including 409 businesses, according to a Department of Defense report to Congress. There were another 443 fraud-related civil cases resulting in judgments against 546 defendants. The value of those contracts exceeded $334 billion, according to the Department of Defense report. During that same period, the Department of Defense entered into more than 15 million contracts with contractors who had been indicted, fined, and/or convicted of fraud, or who reached settlement agreements.

"Simply put, the Pentagon continues to be riddled with waste, fraud, and abuse of taxpayer funds to a degree unmatched across the federal government," Senator Bernard Sanders (D. VT), who was the committee head investigating Department of Defense fraud scandals, said in 2017. "It is unacceptable that the Department of Defense continues to lose vast sums of taxpayer money because of fraud perpetrated by major defense contractors. Procurement fraud includes, but is not limited to, cost and labor mischarging, defective pricing, price fixing, bid rigging, and defective and counterfeit parts," quoted from the report by Department of Defense Inspector General. Senator Sanders added, "This has got to end!" He also said, "The potential damage from procurement fraud extends well beyond finances. This crime poses a serious threat to the Department of Defense's ability to achieve its objectives and can undermine the safety and operational readiness of the warfighter."

**How Do the Big Five Defense Contractors Influence at the Pentagon?**[74]

The Big Five defense contractors have deployed an extremely profitable strategy: recruit armies of lobbyists from former Pentagon officials and congressional staffers who stream through the revolving door. Then, get those former officials to use their relationships and access to influence country's national security apparatus for one purpose — to secure lucrative contracts and boost profits. In 2018 alone, the top 20 defense contractors hired **645 former** senior government officials, top military brass, Members of Congress, and senior legislative staff as lobbyists, board members, or senior executives. **90 percent** of these former officials became registered lobbyists.

Defense contractor influence is a big part of how we ended up with a Pentagon budget that will **cost more** than Ronald Reagan spent at the height of the Cold War. That's more than the federal government spends on education, medical research, border security, housing, the FBI, disaster relief, the State Department, foreign aid — everything else in the discretionary budget put together.

We have to call this what it is: corruption, plain and simple.

---

74 "Reduce Corporate Influence at the Pentagon," Elizabeth Warren, accessed October 19, 2022, https://elizabethwarren.com/plans/corporate-influence-pentagon.

In 2017, Lockheed alone received more than **$35 billion** in taxpayer dollars from defense contracts. That's more than the federal government spent on the entire budget for NASA. Many of these private companies are under pressure to show year over year revenue to their shareholders and investors on Wall Street. That means they are constantly pressuring the federal government for more spending — regardless of our national security needs. It's long past time for real reform.

**Absurd System**[75]

In the years following the 9/11 attacks, the United States and its allies have fought a continuous war on terror. The taxpayer tab for the war totals about $5 trillion, or $16,000 per person, according to Brown University's Watson Institute for International Studies. It was the biggest Pentagon spending buildup in history since World War II. This spending has not only gone into strengthening the U.S. military itself, but also to improving the allied Afghan, Iraqi, and neighboring Middle Eastern security forces. The idea has been to arm Middle Eastern countries to enable them to secure their own territories.

---

[75]Derek Paulhus, "Waste, Greed, and Fraud: The Business That Makes the World's Greatest Army," The Institute of Politics at Harvard University (Harvard Kennedy School), accessed October 19, 2022, https://iop.harvard.edu/get-involved/harvard-political-review/waste-greed-and-fraud-business-makes-world%E2%80%99s-greatest-army.

Billions of dollars' worth of aid have come principally in the form of military contracts. BAE Systems Vice President for External Communications Brian Roehrkasse said in an interview with the HPR that the government determines what products it needs from contractors like BAE. The Pentagon asks primarily for "a lot of combat vehicles," including armored trucks, airplanes, and helicopters.

However, critics like Fareed Zakaria, H.A. Goodman, and Bill Maher point to the rise of ISIS, the retreat of Iraqi security forces, and the incompetence of Middle Eastern forces in general—namely that a combined Middle Eastern military force of four million has been ineffective against an ISIS force of 30,000—as evidence that American military intervention has done little to curb terrorist forces or guarantee allies capable of ensuring peace in the Middle East. In fact, an Institute for Economics and Peace report noted that terrorist attacks were not declining at the hand of the American military and contracting intervention but rather rising sharply.

Reports from the Inspector Generals' offices of Iraq and Afghanistan estimate that the U.S. military has lost $60 billion to waste and fraud in Iraq, $100 billion to Afghan reconstruction efforts, and billions more in wasted equipment either burned or left behind after the withdrawal of forces. Part of the problem may be that the Pentagon has 1.7 million contracts open, which makes oversight difficult, if not impossible.

Another impetus for fraud stems from the blank checks that the Pentagon writes to contractors. The most common method of winning contracts is through the "cost-plus" contracting system, in which the government reimburses contractor expenses and tacks on a commission as profit. According to William Hartung, the Center for International Policy's Arms and Security Project Director, the system works in such a way that "the more work [contractors] do, the more profit they get, even if their work is inefficient. ... It basically says, 'If you spend a billion dollars building a weapons system, you'll get a 10 percent profit or $100 million.'" Essentially, for contractors, "you do better if you are wasteful."

One way defense companies can push for contracts and sell their products is by lobbying the government. In an interview with the HPR, Harvard Kennedy School lecturer Mark Fagan explained that companies lobby to build and articulate strategy on policy issues. He states that defense companies pay large sums of money, sometimes in the form of campaign contributions, to gain the ear of a congressperson or a Pentagon official. Corporations can then influence their member of government to fight against sequester cuts to defense spending, push for their contracts, and more. Such spending has swelled the military industry to become the eighth-largest lobbying sector in the nation, spending well over $100 million annually on lobbying the government. Boeing, Lockheed Martin, Honeywell International, and Northrop Grumman are among the top spenders.

However, while defense companies spend tens of millions of dollars trying to win the ears of politicians, they reap billions in return. U.S.

government defense spending currently totals slightly less than one-fifth of the $3.8 trillion federal budget. While corporate lobbying seems to be at least partially responsible for the bloated defense budget, Fagan argues that defense companies are simply trying to sell their wares to consumers: the government.

Since the 9/11 attacks, America's foreign policy has followed a trend of asserting hasty force instead of deliberative diplomacy. Hartung states that the nation has looked to solve conflicts through force and military means—a policy that has largely backfired. While defense industry marketing to the Pentagon has been partially responsible for the glut and availability of defense equipment and, therefore, the inflated military budget, Fagan pointed out that it is nevertheless "the responsibility of the buyer to make sure that what they are choosing to buy is actually what they need ... [and] it is up to our elected officials ... to determine what is the right course of action for the country's security and for the taxpayers."

Whether these new possibilities come to fruition or not, the Pentagon is trying to ingrain defense spending as a crucial and permanent investment even in times of peace. Although much waste and glut exist within the system, the Pentagon continues to press for even more funds while fighting against calls to decrease the defense budget.

Nevertheless, even if the Pentagon fails to stop defense cuts, contractors are still looking at hundreds of billions in purchases for the Middle East and Africa through 2019 through the DoD's Foreign

Military Sales (FMS) program, a government-to-government sales agreement.

The new conflict in the Middle East is yet another example of the perpetual war that the United States seems to find itself in. As the late Gore Vidal pointed out in his book, *Perpetual War for Perpetual Peace: How We Got to Be So Hated*, the United States always appears to find a new enemy to attack to perpetuate controlled wars, or small conflicts that keep dollars flowing to sustain the defense industry. As Hartung put it, the overriding sentiment in the government has been that "we need [the money] to defend the country, so we can't ask too many questions." When there are calls to cut the defense budget, to withdraw and stop intervening in world conflicts, or to use older equipment available, contractors and lobbyists respond by arguing that the country "needs a new generation of equipment," or that the Pentagon needs to continue a steady stream of purchasing in order "sustain the defense industrial base" to prepare for the next war.

With its blank checks, lack of oversight, and belief that no one should question those contractors and companies that protect the nation, the government has allowed the defense system and contractors to act wastefully, and fraudulent has permitted companies and contractors to take advantage of government spending and has cleared the way for the industry to exercise its influence over the nation's politics in the pursuit of greater profit.

US Navy officer 'bribed by cash and prostitutes'[76]

**A US Navy Commander has pleaded guilty to receiving $250,000 in cash and prostitution services from a foreign defense contractor in exchange for state secrets.**

Information Commander Stephen Shedd provided to the firm helped it defraud the navy of $35m (£26.1m).
The plea is the latest in the 'Fat Leonard' case, considered one of the worst corruption scandals faced by the navy.

Dozens of officials have been ensnared.

Shedd is one of nine members of the Japan-based 7th US fleet indicted by a federal grand jury in March 2017 for their role in the scandal, and the third officer to plead guilty.

According to the Justice Department, Shedd and the other officers received "sex parties with prostitutes and luxurious dinner and travel" in exchange for military secrets and "substantial influence" for the Glenn Defense Marine Asia (GDMA) company, a Singapore-based firm founded by a Malaysian national, Leonard Glenn Francis.

The scandal became widely known as the "Fat Leonard" scheme due to Francis's then-corpulent figure. He was arrested in California after

---

[76] "US Navy Officer 'Bribed by Cash and Prostitutes,'" *BBC News*, January 27, 2022, https://www.bbc.com/news/world-us-canada-60149145.

being lured there by US officials in 2013. He has since pleaded guilty to bribery and conspiracy charges and has remained in prison or home detention.

According to prosecutors, information Shedd and others provided helped GDMA to win and maintain contracts and overbill the Navy by $35m for services such as providing tugboats, security, and waste removal to ships at port.

As part of a plea deal, Shedd admitted that he and the other defendants gave Francis schedules of naval movements and other information and lobbied on behalf of GDMA to other naval officials.

The defendant knew these efforts would result in the service paying GDMA's claims, the Justice Department said.

A total of 34 naval officials, defence contractors and GDMA employees, including Francis, have been charged with crimes related to the scheme. Of these, 28 have pleaded guilty, including two other 7th fleet officers.
Shedd is scheduled to be sentenced on 21 July in a California federal court, while the trial of the remaining six 7th fleet officers is due to begin on 28 February.

**Cases of American Corporate Corruption**

Below are 5 cases that demonstrate American corporate corruption involving the U.S. Government.

**Case: Charlene Shuler Corley**[77]

Charlene Shuler Corley is a former defense contractor who was convicted in 2007 on two counts of conspiracy. Over the course of nine years leading up to September 2006, the company owned by Corley and her sister was found to have received over US$21.5 million from the United States Department of Defense for fraudulent shipping costs; in one instance, the company was paid US$998,798 for shipping two 19-cent washers. In 2009, Corley was sentenced to 78 months in prison and ordered to pay US$15.5 million in restitution.

Along with her twin sister Darlene Shuler Wooten, Corley was the co-owner of C&D Distributors, a supplier of small hardware components, plumbing fixtures and electronic equipment to the military. The company, based in Lexington, South Carolina, used a computerized government system that allowed shipping costs for each order to be submitted separately and automatically reimbursed. Using the system, C&D Distributors received payment from the Department of Defense on 112 fraudulent invoices, totaling US$20.5 million in illegitimate charges, for parts sent to priority military installations, including destinations in Iraq and Afghanistan. The fraud began in 1997 when a mistake on an invoice for shipping charges allowed C&D to make an unexpected profit of US$5,000. Although they returned the money, they discovered that due to a flaw in the system,

---

[77] Renae Merle, "Bad Defense Contractor Was Paid $11 Million Bad to Ship 2 Washers," *The Washington Post,* August 17, 2007, p. D02.

they could charge any amount for shipping and the government would pay it, no questions asked.

Among the invoices submitted by C&D Distributors were:

- US$445,640 for shipping an $8.75 elbow pipe
- US$492,096 for shipping a $10.99 machine thread plug
- US$403,436 for shipping six machine screws worth a total of $59.94

The scheme was discovered in September 2006 when the system red-flagged an invoice for over US$998,000 in shipping charges for washers that only cost 19 cents. A review by a person discovered several of the exorbitant charges. According to a Pentagon spokesman, the system has been modified to safeguard against similar exploitation in the future.

In October 2006, Darlene Wooten committed suicide after being approached by federal investigators. She left behind a suicide note and a check made out to the Department of Defense for US$4.5 million.

Corley and C&D Distributors pled guilty in August 2007 to two conspiracy charges to commit wire fraud and money laundering, each charge carrying a maximum sentence of twenty years. In March 2009, she was sentenced to the minimum recommendation of six and a half years in federal prison. The judge rejected Corley's request to serve the time in a halfway house. Corley was also ordered to pay US$15.5 million in restitution.

**Case: The Cunningham Scandal**[78]

The Cunningham scandal is a U.S. political scandal in which defense contractors paid bribes to members of Congress and officials in the U.S. Defense Department, in return for political favors in the form of federal contracts. Most notable amongst the recipients of the bribes was California Congressman Duke Cunningham who pleaded guilty to receiving over $2.3 million in bribes. The primary defense contractors were Mitchell Wade (owner of MZM) and Brent R. Wilkes (owner of ADCS Inc.).

In June 2005 it was revealed that Wade had bought Cunningham's house in Del Mar for $1,675,000. A month later, Wade placed it back on the market where it remained unsold for 8 months until the price was reduced to $975,000. Cunningham was a member of the Defense Appropriations Subcommittee; soon after the purchase, Wade began to receive tens of millions of dollars' worth of defense and intelligence contracts.

Later in June, it was further reported that the yacht that Cunningham lived on while he was in Washington was owned by Wade, and that Cunningham was paying only for maintenance, not rent. The Federal Bureau of Investigation (FBI) launched an investigation regarding the real estate transaction. Cunningham's home, MZM's Corporate

---

[78] Merle Renae and Smith R. Jeffery, "Pentagon Ends New Work on D.C. Firm's Contract," *The Washington Post*, June 28, 2005.

Offices and Wade's home were all simultaneously raided by a number of federal agencies with warrants on July 1, 2005.

The money and favors provided to Cunningham were in exchange for helping win Pentagon work. "Government procurement records show that MZM, which Wade started in 1993, did not report any revenue from prime contract awards until 2003", but starting in May 2002 they were awarded contracts in the tens of millions of dollars which then grew to well over $150 million.

"Prosecutors also laid out a second, separate conspiracy in which Wade was alleged to have paid bribes to a Defense Department official and other employees in return for their help in awarding contracts to his company. Wade pleaded guilty to this scheme as well. The Pentagon employees were not named in court filings."

On April 27, 2006, Scot J. Patrow, writing for *The Wall Street Journal*, reported prosecutors were investigating whether other members of Congress or their staff received the services of prostitutes provided at Cunningham's request by Mitchell Wade. Patrow also reported that Brent R. Wilkes had indicated that he would fight any charges. Wade implicated Wilkes in the prostitution scheme.
In 1995 Brent R. Wilkes started ADCS Inc. ("Automated Document Conversion Systems"). With Cunningham's help, he began winning contracts from the Pentagon.

As *The Washington Post* put it, "Wilkes was an obscure California contractor and lobbyist until his name surfaced last year as one of two defense contractors alleged to have given Cunningham $2.4

million in cash and other benefits in return for Cunningham's steering government business their way. One of Wilkes's companies received more than $80 million in Pentagon contracts over the past decade that stemmed from earmarks that Cunningham slipped into spending bills."

Cunningham pleaded guilty to federal charges of tax evasion, and conspiracy to commit bribery, mail fraud, and wire fraud. He was sentenced to eight years and four months in prison and was ordered to pay $1.8 million in restitution. On June 4, 2013, Cunningham completed his prison sentence; he now lives in Arkansas.

Wilkes was convicted on November 5, 2007, on all 13 counts of conspiracy, bribery, money laundering, and wire fraud. With his court appeals exhausted, Wilkes surrendered to federal marshals in San Antonio, Texas, to serve his 12-year-sentence. Mitchell Wade, another contractor who bribed Cunningham, pleaded guilty and ended up testifying against Wilkes, receiving a 30-month sentence.

### Operation Ill Wind[79]

Operation Ill Wind was a three-year investigation launched in 1986 by the United States Federal Bureau of Investigation into corruption by U.S. government and military officials, and private defense contractors. Charles "Chuck" Duff was the sole Air Force Action Officer responsible for developing,

---

[79] Marquis Christopher, "M. R. Paisley, 77, Dies; Bid-Rigging Figure," *The New York Times*, December 26, 2001.

coordinating, and implementing Air Force actions relating to the Department of Justice's "Ill Wind" procurement fraud investigation. Government officials, private individuals, and companies were eventually convicted of various crimes, including nine government officials, 42 Washington consultants, and 7 military contractors, as well as executives at GE, Boeing, and United Technologies.

Melvyn Paisley, appointed Assistant Secretary of the Navy in 1981 by Republican President Ronald Reagan, was found to have accepted hundreds of thousands of dollars in bribes. He pleaded guilty to bribery and served four years in prison.

James E. Gaines, Deputy Assistant Secretary of the Navy, took over when Paisley resigned his office. Gaines was convicted of accepting an illegal gratuity and theft and conversion of government property. He was sentenced to six months in prison.

Victor D. Cohen, Deputy Assistant Secretary of the Air Force, was the 50th conviction obtained under the Ill Wind probe when he pleaded guilty to accepting bribes and conspiring to defraud the government.

Most worked for Unisys, pleading guilty to eight felonies, including the use of fraud, bribery, and illegal campaign contributions to obtain billions of dollars in defense contracts. Other top officials worked for Lee Telecommunications and Teledyne.

The scandal led the United States Congress to pass the 1988 Procurement Integrity Act, which regulates the pay that procurement officials can receive from contractors during the first year after they leave the government and forbids them from providing bid and proposal information to their new employers.

**Vice President Dick Cheney's Profits from the Iraq War**[80]

The Costs of War Project by the Watson Institute for International Studies at Brown University said the war in Iraq cost $1.7 trillion dollars, not including the $490 billion in immediate benefits owed to veterans of the war and the lifetime benefits that will be owed to them or their next of kin. Former Halliburton subsidiary received $39.5 billion in Iraq-related contracts over the war years. George W. Bush's Vice President Dick Cheney Joined Halliburton in 1995 as Chief Executive Officer and served as CEO until 2000. Cheney resigned as CEO on the same day he was announced as George Bush's vice-presidential pick in the 2000 election.

The accounting of the financial cost of the nearly decade-long Iraq War will go on for years, but a recent analysis has shed light on the companies that made money off the war by providing support services as the privatization of what were former U.S. military operations rose to unprecedented levels. Private or publicly listed firms received at least $138 billion of U.S. taxpayer money for

---

[80] Angelo Young, *International Business Times.*

government contracts for services that included providing private security, building infrastructure, and feeding the troops.

Ten contractors received 52 percent of the funds, according to an analysis by the *Financial Times* that was published Tuesday. The No. 1 recipient? Houston-based energy-focused engineering and construction firm KBR, Inc. (NYSE: KBR), which was spun off from its parent, oilfield services provider Halliburton Co. (NYSE: HAL), in 2007 and whose CEO was Dick Cheney. The company was given $39.5 billion in Iraq-related contracts over the past decade, with many of the deals given without any bidding from competing firms, such as a $568-million contract renewal in 2010 to provide housing, meals, water, and bathroom services to soldiers, a deal that led to a Justice Department lawsuit over alleged kickbacks, as reported by *Bloomberg*.

The Justice Department said pursued a lawsuit accusing the Houston-based company of taking kickbacks from two subcontractors on Iraq-related work. The Army also awarded the work to KBR over objections from members of Congress, who have pushed the Pentagon to seek bids for further logistics contracts. Halliburton agreed to pay $13.67 million to settle a whistleblower lawsuit alleging that its employees accepted kickbacks while providing logistics support to U.S. Army forces in the Middle East.

The lawsuit accused employees of the Houston-based Kellogg Brown & Root (KBR, subsidiary of Halliburton) of rigging contracts and overcharging the government in Iraq and Afghanistan. The company resolved the lawsuit without admitting liability.

## Legal Corruption in America

There are numerous more cases of corporate corruption in America, too numerous to go through in this book. Let us now turn to two cases (of many) that involve legal corruption in America.

Legal corruption occurs when the laws of a country sanction the corruption of oligarchs and other individuals or parties who can profit from the seemingly unfair laws of the country.

## Citizens United v. Federal Election Commission[81]

The Supreme Court's ruling in *Citizens United v. Federal Election Commission* in 2010 was a controversial decision that reversed century-old campaign finance restrictions and enabled corporations and other outside groups to spend unlimited funds on elections.

While wealthy donors, corporations, and special interest groups have long had an outsized influence in elections, and that sway has dramatically expanded since the *Citizens United* decision, with negative repercussions for American democracy and the fight against political corruption.

---

[81] Tim Lau, "Citizens United Explained," Brennan Center for Justice, December 12, 2019, https://www.brennancenter.org/our-work/research-reports/citizens-united-explained.

What was *Citizens United* about? A conservative nonprofit group called Citizens United challenged campaign finance rules after the FEC stopped it from promoting and airing a film criticizing presidential candidate Hillary Clinton too close to the presidential primaries. A 5–4 majority of the Supreme Court sided with Citizens United, ruling that corporations and other outside groups can spend unlimited money on elections.

In the court's opinion, Justice Anthony Kennedy wrote that limiting "independent political spending" from corporations and other groups violates the First Amendment right to free speech. The justices who voted with the majority assumed that independent spending cannot be corrupt and that the spending would be transparent, but both assumptions have proven to be incorrect.

With its decision, the Supreme Court overturned election spending restrictions that date back more than 100 years. Previously, the court had upheld certain spending restrictions, arguing that the government had a role in preventing corruption. But in *Citizens United*, a bare majority of the justices held that "independent political spending" did not present a substantive threat of corruption, provided it was not coordinated with a candidate's campaign.

As a result, corporations can now spend unlimited funds on campaign advertising if they are not formally "coordinating" with a candidate or political party.

How has *Citizens United* changed elections in the United States?

The ruling has ushered in massive increases in political spending from outside groups, dramatically expanding the already outsized political influence of wealthy donors, corporations, and special interest groups.

In the immediate aftermath of the *Citizens United* decision, analysts focused much of their attention on how the Supreme Court designated corporate spending on elections as free speech. But perhaps the most significant outcomes of *Citizens United* have been the creation of super PACs, which empower the wealthiest donors, and the expansion of dark money through shadowy nonprofits that don't disclose their donors.

A Brennan Center report by Daniel I. Weiner pointed out that a very small group of Americans now wield "more power than at any time since Watergate, while many of the rest seem to be disengaging from politics."

"This is perhaps the most troubling result of *Citizens United*: in a time of historic wealth inequality," wrote Weiner, "the decision has helped reinforce the growing sense that our democracy primarily serves the interests of the wealthy few, and that democratic participation for the vast majority of citizens is of relatively little value."

An election system that is skewed heavily toward wealthy donors also sustains racial bias and reinforces the racial wealth gap. *Citizens United* also unleashed political spending from special interest groups.

**What are PACs and super PACs?**

Political action committees, or "PACs," are organizations that raise and spend money for campaigns that support or oppose political candidates, legislation, or ballot initiatives. Traditional PACs are permitted to donate directly to a candidate's official campaign, but they are also subject to contribution limits, both in terms of what they can receive from individuals and what they can give to candidates. For example, PACs are only permitted to contribute up to $5,000 per year to a candidate per election.

In the 2010 case *Speechnow.org v. FEC*, however, a federal appeals court ruled — applying logic from *Citizens United* — that outside groups could accept unlimited contributions from both individual donors and corporations as long as they don't give directly to candidates. Labeled "super PACs," these outside groups were still permitted to spend money on independently produced ads and on other communications that promote or attack specific candidates.

In other words, super PACs are not bound by spending limits on what they can collect or spend. Additionally, super PACs are required to disclose their donors, but those donors can include dark money groups, which make the original source of the donations unclear. And while super PACs are technically prohibited from coordinating directly with candidates, weak coordination rules have often proven ineffective.

Super PAC money started influencing elections almost immediately after *Citizens United*. From 2010 to 2018, super PACs spent approximately $2.9 billion on federal elections. Notably, the bulk of that money comes from just a few wealthy individual donors. In the 2018 election cycle, for example, the top 100 donors to super PACs contributed nearly 78 percent of all super PAC spending.

What is dark money?

Dark money is election-related spending where the source is secret. *Citizens United* contributed to a major jump in this type of spending, which often comes from nonprofits that are not required to disclose their donors.

In its decision, the Supreme Court reasoned that unlimited spending by wealthy donors and corporations would not distort the political process, because the public would be able to see who was paying for ads and "give proper weight to different speakers and messages." But in reality, the voters often cannot know who is actually behind campaign spending.

That's because leading up to *Citizens United*, transparency in U.S. elections had started to erode, thanks to a disclosure loophole opened by the Supreme Court's 2007 ruling in *FEC v. Wisconsin Right to Life*, along with inaction by the IRS and controversial rulemaking by the FEC.

*Citizens United* allowed big political spenders to exploit the growing lack of transparency in political spending. This has contributed to a surge in secret spending from outside groups in federal elections. Dark money expenditures increased from less than $5 million in 2006 to more than $300 million in the 2012 election cycle and more than $174 million in the 2014 midterms. In the top 10 most competitive 2014 Senate races, more than 71 percent of the outside spending on the winning candidates was dark money. These numbers actually underestimate the impact of dark money on recent elections, because they do not include super PAC spending that may have originated with dark money sources, or spending that happens outside the "electioneering communications window" 30 days before a primary or 60 days before a general election.

Finally, because they can hide the identities of their donors, dark money groups also provide a way for foreign countries to hide their activity from U.S. voters and law enforcement agencies. This increases the vulnerability of U.S. elections to international interference.

## Redistricting[82]

Redistricting is another form of legal corruption practiced in America because it is a legal method to gain political and financial gain through oftentimes unethical but legal means. Redistricting is the process of drawing electoral district boundaries within a state. *The Uniform Congressional District Act* (enacted in 1967) requires that representatives be elected from single-member districts. When a state has a single representative, that district will be state-wide and affective in state and federal voting and financial priorities.

[82] Annika Kim Constantino, "Gerrymandering Could Limit Minority Voters' Power Even Though Census Shows Population Gains," *CNBC*, August 13, 2021, https://www.cnbc.com/2021/08/13/gerrymandering-could-limit-minority-voters-power-even-after-census-gains.html.

Redistricting has become subject to contentious political debate over the years with critics arguing that it has been weaponized to neutralize minority voting power, as well as provide unequal electoral votes to either Democrats or Republicans, based on which party is in power during a redistricting process. Supporters say it enhances electoral competitiveness, of course for their own purposes.

Each state can set its own standards for Congressional and legislative districts. In addition to equalizing the population of districts and complying with federal requirements, criteria may include attempting to create compact, contiguous districts, trying to keep political units and communities within a single district, and avoiding the drawing of boundaries for purposes of partisan advantage or incumbent protection.

Redistricting may follow other criteria depending on state and local laws:

1. compactness
2. contiguity
3. equal population
4. preservation of existing political communities
5. partisan fairness
6. racial fairness

## Gerrymandering

The term gerrymandering is named after American politician Elbridge Gerry, Vice President of the United States at the time of his death, who, as Governor of Massachusetts in 1812, signed a bill that created a partisan district in the Boston area that was compared to the shape of a mythological salamander.

Today, the pejorative term gerrymandering is no longer used to describe politically and financially motivated redistricting. Gerrymandering, the practice of drawing district boundaries to achieve political divisions that are advantageous for legislators of a particular political party, and involves the manipulation of district boundaries to leave out, or include, specific populations in a particular district to ensure a legislator's reelection or to advantage their party.

In states where the legislature (or another body where a partisan majority is possible) is in charge of redistricting, the possibility of gerrymandering (the deliberate manipulation of political boundaries for electoral advantage, usually of incumbents or a specific political party) often makes the process very politically contentious, especially when the majorities of the two houses of the legislature, or the legislature and the governor, are from different parties.

Partisan domination of state legislatures and improved technology to design contiguous districts that pack opponents into as few districts as possible has led to district maps that are skewed towards one party. Consequently, many states, including Florida, Georgia, Maryland, Michigan, N.Carolina, Ohio, Pennsylvania, Texas, and Wisconsin have succeeded in reducing or effectively eliminating competition for most House seats in those states. Some states, including New Jersey and New York, protect incumbents of both parties by reducing the number of competitive districts.

The state and federal court systems are often involved in resolving disputes over Congressional and legislative redistricting when gridlock prevents redistricting in a timely manner. In addition, those disadvantaged by a proposed redistricting plan may challenge it in state and federal courts. Justice Department approval (which is known as pre-clearance) was formerly required under Section 5 of the Voting Rights Act of 1965 in certain states that have had a history of racial barriers to voting. The Supreme Court's ruling on the Pennsylvania redistricting effectively allows elected officials to select their constituents by eliminating most of the grounds for constituents to challenge district lines.

## U.S. Supreme Court Redistricting Cases

While state courts have been used to challenge and settle redistricting. The U.S. Supreme Court has been summoned to resolve redistricting cases that could not be settled on the state level. Here it should be noted separately another well-known legal corruption that exists in America, that of U.S. presidents appointing judges to the Supreme Court who lean in the direction of that president's party preferences in areas such as social justice, corporate law, women's rights, and other contentious issues.

Redistricting cases that were brought up in State Supreme Courts are far too numerous to list here. However, below is a partial list of Supreme Court cases that were judged by the highest Federal court in the land regarding redistricting cases.

Colegrove v. Green (1946), Baker v. Carr (1962), Gray v. Sanders (1963), Wesberry v. Sanders (1964), Burns v. Richardson (1966), Reynolds v. Sims (1964), Gaffney v. Cummings (1973), Karcher v. Daggett (1983), Thornburg v. Gingles (1986), Davis v. Bandemer (1986), Growe v. Emison (1993), Voinovich v. Quilter (1993), Shaw v. Reno (1993), Johnson v. DeGrandy (1994), Miller v. Johnson (1995), Bush v. Vera (1996), Hunt v. Cromartie (1999), Vieth v. Jubelirer (2004), League of United Latin American Citizens v. Perry (2006), Bartlett v. Strickland (2009), Arizona State Legislature v. Arizona Independent Redistricting Commission (2015), Gill v. Whitford (2018), Benisek v. Lamone (2018 & 2019), Rucho v. Common Cause (2019)

## Conclusions

We have investigated and examined illegal and legal corruption in America. We have made comparisons with Transparency International's index. Unfortunately, this agency has many scandals and has been faulty. Is America as corrupt as South Sudan? Is America corrupt too broad of a question? There is corruption in America. There have been and will be corrupt men and women in

America who seek personal gain through fraudulent government contracts, oligarch connections, or through legal means such as Supreme Court decisions that favor redistricting for personal political and financial gain. There are currently 330 million Americans. What percentage of the population is corrupt? There are some who call America a kleptocracy. This is very difficult to prove, though, of course, there are records of large thefts in America, as we have documented. We have not even delved into the corrupt theft of the lands of the American indigenous people and their genocide at the hands of European and American White people. Others call Russia a kleptocracy. What is the proof of that? Is Iran really a theocracy?

It is dangerous to stereotype one country by one characteristic. The danger lies in the fact that others may use that characterization for the promotion of misunderstanding and conflict. Hitler stereotyped the Jews, and we know what happened from that action. There are Muslims that believe all non-Muslims are infidels and should be converted or killed. History is full of these types of single and pernicious characterizations or stereotypes. These have never led to peace.

The solution to ending corruption in any country is to create and maintain fair and just laws that benefit all, rich and poor, of every race, religion and culture. Fair and just laws are the basis for the moral ethos of any great nation. The second president of the United States said, “America is a land governed by laws, not men.” This is a great ideal for any nation. Men are corruptible but laws are not. Let America continue to make just and fair laws and abide by those laws in the spirit that they were created for the good. Let America abide by international laws and rules and not by corrupted political or imperialistic goals. And let us all teach our children to learn, understand and abide by the highest good and the most ideal ethics. And let us stay vigilant about America in the world's affairs and continue to urge the behavior of America to move toward the highest good for all.

## Bibliography

"Bad Defense Contractor Was Paid $I1 Million Bad to Ship 2 Washers." *The Washington Post*, August 17, 2007.

Christopher, Marquis. "M. R. Paisley, 77, Dies; Bid-Rigging Figure." *The New York Times*, December 26, 2001.

Constantino, Annika Kim. "Gerrymandering Could Limit Minority Voters' Power Even Though Census Shows Population Gains." *CNBC*, August 13, 2021. https://www.cnbc.com/2021/08/13/gerrymandering-could-limit-minority-voters-power-even-after-census-gains.html.

Editor. "Transparency International Strips United States Affiliate of Accreditation." *Corporate Crime Reporter*, January 19, 2017. https://www.corporatecrimereporter.com/news/200/transparency-international-strips-us-affiliate-of-accreditation/.

"Integrity Initiative." siemens.com Global Website. Accessed October 19, 2022. http://www.siemens.com/.

"Is Transparency International's Measure of Corruption Still Valid?" *The Guardian*, December 3, 2013. https://www.theguardian.com/global-development/poverty-matters/2013/dec/03/transparency-international-measure-corruption-valid.

Lau, Tim. "Citizens United Explained." Brennan Center for Justice, December 12, 2019. https://www.brennancenter.org/our-work/research-reports/citizens-united-explained.

Mier, Brian. "Transparency International: Brazil Court Opens Investigation of Anti-Corruption NGO." *BRASILWIRE,* April 14, 2022. https://www.brasilwire.com/brazils-auditing-court-opens-investigation-against-transparency-international/.

Paulhus, Derek. "Waste, Greed, and Fraud: The Business That Makes the World's Greatest Army." The Institute of Politics at Harvard University. Harvard Kennedy School. Accessed October 19, 2022. https://iop.harvard.edu/get-involved/harvard-political-review/waste-greed-and-fraud-business-makes-world%E2%80%99s-greatest-army.

"Reduce Corporate Influence at the Pentagon." Elizabeth Warren. Accessed October 19, 2022. https://elizabethwarren.com/plans/corporate-influence-pentagon.

Renae, Merle, and Smith R. Jeffery. "Pentagon Ends New Work on D.C. Firm's Contract." *The Washington Post*, June 28, 2005.

Richter, Frederik. "Falling on Deaf Ears." correctiv.org, August 27, 2015. https://correctiv.org/en/latest-stories/corruption/2015/08/27/falling-on-deaf-ears/.

"Transparency International Statement on Its Former Chapter in Croatia." Transparency International, April 12, 2016. https://www.transparency.org/en/press/transparency-international-statement-on-its-former-chapter-in-croatia.

"US Navy Officer 'Bribed by Cash and Prostitutes.'" *BBC News*, January 27, 2022. https://www.bbc.com/news/world-us-canada-60149145.

Vidhi, Doshi. "Transparency International Staff Complain of Bullying and Harassment." *The Guardian*, August 21, 2019. https://www.theguardian.com/global-development/2019/aug/21/transparency-international-staff-complain-of-bullying-harassment.

## About the Author

Nate Reztirob (American, 1950-) is a scholar of international history, global diplomacy, and conflicts from the early 19th century to the current times. His areas of expertise include the Cold War era, official secrecy, colonial struggles, and revolution. He has written extensive articles on international and domestic politics for magazines and periodicals. Professor Reztirob has taught at Columbia University and in the Department of History of the Gerald R. Ford School of Public Policy at the University of Michigan. He has also been a visiting professor at the Institut d'Etudes Politiques de Paris (Sciences), the University of Oslo, and the University of Sydney. His work employs novel and innovative approaches to historical study, including examining the past through a global or transnational lens and applying data-mining techniques to historical research.

Made in the USA
Las Vegas, NV
10 July 2023

74429381R00144